Shepherd's London

Shepherd's London

J F C Phillips

BOOK CLUB ASSOCIATES
LONDON

To my wife, Veronica

Title page Wood engraving (British Museum: Crace Collection, XXXVIII) prepared *c* 1842 for *A Diorama of London*, an apparently unpublished work by T. H. Shepherd. It suggests what he looked like, although showing him as a painter in oils rather than with his normal equipment of sketch pad and pencil.

This edition published 1976 by
Book Club Associates
By arrangement with Cassell & Co. Ltd

Copyright © John Phillips 1976

First published 1976

Designed by Kathryn S. A. Booth

Filmset and printed in Great Britain by
BAS Printers Limited, Wallop, Hampshire

Contents

Foreword   6

Author's Preface   7

The Shepherds and their London   8

Plates and Text   16

Map of London in 1832   100

A Guide to the Shepherds' London Drawings   102

The Major Collections   108

Bibliography   110

Appendix   112

Notes   113

Index   115

Foreword

Stanley Spencer once remarked to me that the making of a record was as good a reason for painting as any other. Though this unpremeditated *obiter dictum* might fail to pass muster in the more rarified art circles, being at once too professional and reach me down, like Turner's 'Anything will do for a subject', it is nonetheless true. Nor is a pictorial record a thing so easy of accomplishment: it is extremely difficult even to do a matter of fact, unimaginative, topographical drawing, let alone one which will vividly evoke a sense of place and specific local character and convey the artist's emotions. Beyond question, English topographical art, from its dim beginnings at the time of Hollar, and English topographical artists of all ranks have served us well. We may not have produced much to rival the views of old Paris by Meryon, in which superb draughtsmanship is linked with an almost overwhelming mood of strangeness and undertones of disquiet, but we have produced a vast body of most admirable work, to which we owe our knowledge of the appearance of London and other English towns and cities in the eighteenth century and particularly in the nineteenth century, when a fortunate combination of circumstances made the general distribution of these records possible. This was first the existence of many gifted topographical artists like the Shepherd family, the introduction of steel engraving to replace engraving on copper, and lastly a public with an appetite for topographical publications whetted by the Romantic movement; kept from Continental travel by the Napoleonic wars, they turned their interests inwardly, as it were, on the scenery and buildings of the homeland.

Without these drawings and the engravings made from them, we should have only the most imprecise notions of what London looked like before *Metropolitan Improvements* of a later and more vandalistic kind came to pass; we should, for example, be in the dark about the appearance of the vanished Wren churches of the City. In this tremendous topographical production, the Shepherd family, especially T. H. Shepherd, played a prominent part, doing for London what Harwood, Pyne, Pickering and Allom did for the provinces. Hardly a book can be written nowadays on nineteenth-century London without using a Shepherd illustration.

John Phillips's book, a model of plain writing and considerable scholarship, pays this topographical family the compliment their labours deserve. It also acts as a guide to the identification of their originals, and in addition gives us much interesting information about the buildings the Shepherds drew. What is more, it does what books should do: it prompts one to action, to find out more about the Shepherds, to collect their engraved publications and to get to know more about London.

Geoffrey Fletcher

Preface

Thomas Hosmer Shepherd is a paradox. His pictures are very well-known—indeed, they have formed our image of Regency London. They can be found in almost every book concerned with some aspect of London in the nineteenth century. They are the most popular items in print shops, and are endlessly reproduced on table-mats and biscuit-boxes. Yet until recently he has been a shadowy figure—even the dates of his birth and death were unknown.

It was Thomas Hosmer's colourful late watercolours, standing out from the generally more sober contents of the Greater London Council Print Collection, which first drew my attention and then made me aware of the lack of information about an artist on whose work we rely so heavily for our knowledge of London. What began as a study of Thomas Hosmer soon broadened to include the three other artists of the same name, George, George Sidney and Frederick, with whom it became clear he was connected. The Shepherds remain anonymous—not a single personal document other than their drawings survives—but from ratebooks, parish registers, exhibition catalogues and census records a pattern has emerged which justifies our reliance on their work. But their pictures are more than an industrious chronicle of their surroundings. They reveal *Shepherd's London*, which both resembles and differs from the London of Dickens and Mayhew.

Many individuals and institutions have assisted in the writing of this book. My thanks are due to the Greater London Council and to my colleagues in the Greater London Record Office, in particular the former Head Archivist, Miss E. D. Mercer. I have drawn heavily on the resources of the Council's Library. Mr B. S. Johnson gave me the valuable notes on the Shepherd family prepared by him for Captain Jack Gilbey, which he had originally given to Dr F. H. W. Sheppard who generously waived his interest in them. Mr Bernard Adams made freely available his bibliography of the Shepherds' published work and his valuable analysis of the printing history of *Metropolitan Improvements*. Mr Eric Willats, Islington Reference Librarian, gave me the benefit of his own research into the Shepherds' connections with the area. I have been greatly helped by the staff of the various London collections containing Shepherd drawings, notably Miss Joan Pollard of the Museum of London, Mr Ralph Hyde of the Guildhall Library, Miss M. J. Swarbrick and her colleagues in the Archives Department, Westminster City Libraries, and Mr B. Curle who is responsible for the Kensington Local History Collection. Mr R. Winder of Messrs. C. Hoare and Co., Mr N. K. Grace, Dr J. E. C. Peters, Mr P. Jackson, Dr John Hayes and the staffs of the National Army Museum, the National Maritime Museum and the Port of London Authority have all contributed information and advice.

Finally, I must record four major debts: to Mr Paul Lewis, who originally suggested the format of *Shepherd's London*, to my publishers, who took up the idea, to Mr Geoffrey Fletcher, who generously agreed to contribute the foreword, and to my wife, whose encouragement and support of the project at every stage culminated in her typing of the manuscript.

Balham, May 1975

The Shepherds and their London

On Tuesday, 19 March 1878 Frederick Shepherd, artist, aged 58, died in the infirmary of St Luke's workhouse, City Road.[1] He had been admitted to Gray's Inn Road casual ward in June 1876 and transferred to City Road the following October,[2] probably already crippled by the paralysis from which he died. With him died the Shepherd tradition of topographical draughtsmanship, on which so much of our knowledge of Regency and early Victorian London depends.

The story began 85 years earlier and 500 yards away across City Road, at the parish church of St Luke, Old Street, where on 24 February 1793 a young artist named George Shepherd and his wife Nancy brought their six week old son Thomas Hosmer to be baptised.[3] George's own origins are obscure, although there is a suggestion that he was born in Hertfordshire or Bedfordshire.[4] However, the family's movements early in 1793 are thrown into sharp relief by the search-light of world history. When Thomas Hosmer was born on 16 January they were living in France;[5] this may account for the shadowy connection with France which recurs at intervals during Thomas Hosmer's later life. Five days after Thomas Hosmer's birth, Louis XVI was guillotined, and on 1 February France declared war on Great Britain. This no doubt prompted the Shepherds' hasty return to England, and by the middle of February they had settled on the northern outskirts of London, in a modest neighbourhood close to the City Road.

Thomas Hosmer's subsequent career was clearly affected by his early environment. The City Road was a good area for a growing family—inexpensive, healthy and quiet; it was also one of the parts of London where change was most in evidence. The City Road itself was the easternmost section of London's first bypass, designed to enable travellers to and from the City to avoid the narrow and crowded streets of Westminster. When completed about 1770 it ran from the high ground at the Angel, Islington down through fields and market gardens to the edge of the built-up area near Bunhill Fields. By providing access to considerable areas of cheaper land, the laying-out of the City Road stimulated development, and by the 1790's speculative building of a modest kind was spreading northwards beyond St Luke's, Old Street. Yet there were still market gardens nearby in 1814 (pl. 4), and the village of Islington was only ten minutes' walk away. Thomas Hosmer's drawings reflect an enduring affection for the scenes of his childhood—the robust lines of St Luke's Hospital, the unmistakable fluted spire of the church, Peerless Pool where he must often have swum, the mellow simplicity of Alleyn's almshouses (pls. 17, 36). He was familiar from the first with the juxtaposition of old and new in the changing London which it was to be his life's work to record.

During the first ten years of the nineteenth century George Shepherd steadily built up a reputation as an architectural and topographical draughtsman. He appears to have developed late: the earliest drawing of a London subject which I have been able to trace is dated 1801,[6] when he must have been over 30, to judge from the date of Thomas Hosmer's birth. The award to him in 1803 and 1804 of the Society of Arts' silver palettes for drawings of St Albans and Canterbury shows that he was still regarded as a promising newcomer. By the time that George and

Nancy's only other known child, George Sidney, was born, *c.* 1801/1802,[7] his father had begun to send works to the Royal Academy, giving his address as 3 Ratcliff Row, City Road. He exhibited at the Academy regularly from 1800 to 1811, but probably derived his main income from an increasing flow of commissions from publishers of illustrated topography.

George Shepherd's frequent changes of address after 1808, when he left Ratcliff Row, indicate an increasing if precarious prosperity. From 1808 until 1814 he appears to have occupied rented accommodation at three successive addresses[8] in the neighbourhood of Fitzroy Square. This deliberate move westwards into what was then one of the principal artists' quarters brought him into close proximity with many of the best-known painters of the day, although evidence of his contacts with them is lacking. He worked extremely hard during these years, building up a stock of topographical drawings; most of his drawings of London subjects were produced between 1809 and 1811. Of those which were subsequently engraved, many were not published until several years later; he may have disposed of them progressively during the years 1812 to 1820 when he did not exhibit at the Academy and was beginning to undertake sketching tours in the south and west of England. In 1813 he began to collaborate with his elder son, the 20 year old Thomas Hosmer, on a series of aquatints of London street scenes for the publisher Ackermann's *Repository of the Arts*, to which Thomas Hosmer first contributed as early as 1809. By August 1814 the family could afford to move across the Euston Road to a newly-built house, 2 Euston (now Melton) Street, Euston Square.

In 1814 the Euston Road was not the boundary that it has since become. The Act of 1756 which sanctioned the laying-out of the New Road laid down that new building along it was to be set back at least 50 feet from the roadway, with the result that by 1820 a succession of well-mannered terraces lined the section between Regent's Park and King's Cross. The sequence was broken by Euston Square, a spacious conception in which the road was flanked to north and south by ample gardens. In 1814 the transformation which the coming of the railway would bring north of the Euston Road still lay in the unimaginable future. Early in 1817 George moved again, probably seeking more space and a pleasant situation, to 9 Clarendon (now Werrington) Street, a more substantial house with a rateable value of £30 facing across the fields of Rhodes Farm. This was in Somers Town, a district which had not realised the hopes of those who had tried to promote it as a fashionable suburb in the 1790's. Instead it had attracted people in search of inexpensive accommodation, including a sizeable population of French emigrés. In 1822 George took a still larger house nearby, rated at £42, 10 Clarendon Square. These years saw his first recorded sketching tours: in 1812, possibly 1813, 1816 and 1818/19 he visited Bedfordshire,[9] and in 1817 the area around Rye in Sussex.[10] The tour for which most evidence survives took place in the summer of 1819; starting probably from the Reading area in mid-July, George went up the Kennet valley to Hungerford, turned north into Oxfordshire as far as Banbury and returned to London in October.[11]

Meanwhile George's elder son was already making his mark. In 1809, at the age of 16, Thomas Hosmer produced a drawing of East India House[12] which was published as an aquatint in the *Repository* in March 1810. This juvenile work contains few hints of his mature style. The next drawing which I have been able to trace (pl. 20) shows his father's influence both in the choice of subject and in his treatment of it. In the series of street scenes for Ackermann, however, he was already beginning to move away from George's preoccupation with largely antiquarian themes. In 1816 he emerged from his apprenticeship with the first of a series of six major views of London. In each of these, measuring approximately 340×480 mm, an impressively detailed representation of an important public building is carefully complemented by a spirited street scene (pls. 8, 12). The aquatints produced from these are among the most splendid ever issued by Ackermann; they were prepared by three leading engravers, William Havell, J. C. Stadler and J. Bluck.

About 1818, no doubt partly on the strength of this successful commission, Thomas Hosmer married: nothing is known of his bride, Jane Maria, beyond the fact that she was 21 and came originally from Caernarvonshire.[5] Their honeymoon apparently took them to France, to judge from a remarkable watercolour[13] which dates from the late summer of 1818; this watercolour shows the unfinished column marking the site on the cliffs near Boulogne where Napoleon's Grande Armée had encamped some 14 years earlier. When on 8 June 1819 the Shepherds' first child was born,[14] they named him Frederick Napoleon.

By 1820 the young family had set up their own home in Chapman Street, Islington,[15] one of several new streets off the west side of Liverpool Road. Here they were on the very edge of the built-up area; to the north stretched the largely untouched fields of Barnsbury, while westwards open ground fell away steeply towards St Pancras and the new Regent's Canal. Nevertheless, most of London could be seen from the nearby heights of Pentonville, and Somers Town was little more than a mile away. Chapman Street is now Batchelor Street, but number 26 still survives, a modest three-storey terrace house in which the Shepherds lived until about 1841. They probably knew the drawing-master and topographical artist John Hassell (1767–1825), who lived in Richard Street, the next turning off Liverpool Road; Thomas Hosmer contributed plates to his last publication, *Excursions of Pleasure . . .* (1823).

Thomas Hosmer's work over the next three years consisted of bread-and-butter topographical drawings, for Wilkinson's *Londina Illustrata* in particular. His drawing of the interior of St Bartholomew the Great[16] (May 1821) shows a young artist seated sketch book in hand, probably a self-portrait. Tantalisingly, his face is turned away, and all that can be seen is a head of thick dark hair and a vivid blue coat. At about this time Ackermann commissioned more large drawings from him, and published three of them as aquatints (pl. 15) in 1822. Two are of Regent Street and give an interesting foretaste of *Metropolitan Improvements*. In 1825 they were followed by a further series of large aquatints, *A Picturesque Tour on the Regent's Canal* (pl. 17).

Thomas Hosmer must have left home by about 1818, but his younger brother George Sidney continued to live with their father in Somers Town until his own marriage about 1831. During Thomas Hosmer's formative years George was still concerned primarily with straightforward topographical drawing, but by the time that George Sidney was growing up he had begun to paint landscapes and marine subjects as well as topography. In 1821 he began to exhibit again at the Royal Academy, showing views of south Devon which he had probably visited for the first time in the previous year. During the next few years he and George Sidney spent periods there, near Ivybridge, but Thomas Hosmer never seems to have accompanied them. Between then and 1830 George exhibited a further five times at the Academy and four times at the Society of British Artists. To judge from the exhibition lists, he and his younger son influenced each other considerably, particularly in the direction of genre subjects which George showed for the first time at the S.B.A. in 1830 (the last time he ever exhibited), when they were fast becoming one of George Sidney's favourite themes. A tendency to experiment is a marked characteristic of George's work towards the end of his life; in the late 1820's, perhaps stimulated by Thomas Hosmer's achievements, he returned to London topography with a series of tiny vignettes of London, measuring a mere 60 × 100 mm (pl. 26). These gem-like works show no signs of failing powers, but George completely disappears from view in 1831, when he left 10 Clarendon Square. He may have gone to live with George Sidney, who married about that time, but he must by then have been aged over sixty and may well have died before the end of the 1830's.

Before his death George saw his elder son rapidly become the best-known topographical artist of his day. In 1826 Jones and Co., enterprising publishers who were shortly to take over the famous firm of Lackington and Allen, conceived the idea of an illustrated publication, to be issued in parts, which would depict the many new buildings and streets of Regency London under the title of *Metropolitan Improvements*. They may have been inspired by Britton and Pugin's *Public Buildings of London*, which began to appear in 1825; while primarily architectural in emphasis, this contained elegant street views. By using the recently perfected technique of steel engraving illustrated works could now be produced in larger and therefore cheaper editions, and *Metropolitan Improvements* was designed to appeal to a wide readership. As the title-page makes clear, the 159 plates were the most important part of the book, although the accompanying text by the architect and historian James Elmes was by no means negligible. As artist, Thomas Hosmer proved to be the ideal choice—experienced, used to working with engravers, and evidently able to work under pressure.

He began the drawings for *Metropolitan Improvements* in 1826, and the first of its 41 parts, price one shilling, appeared the following year. It was a tremendous success; in March 1829 a reviewer of *Cheap Topographical Publications* in the *Gentleman's Magazine* wrote that 'the great demand for the Views of the *Metropolitan Improvements* . . . has induced many publishers to embark on similar works . . .', one of which was Pugin's *Paris* (1831). However, the first to follow up this success were Jones and Co. themselves, and from 1826 until 1831 they appear to have monopolised Thomas Hosmer's pencil.

During 1827, while continuing to work on *Metropolitan Improvements*, he spent considerable periods in the West Country and Scotland[17] making sketches for two further volumes, *Bath and Bristol . . . displayed . . .* and *Modern Athens* (Edinburgh), each with text by the well-known antiquary John Britton. In 1828 he must have been fully occupied in working up his sketches for these three publications, but somehow found time to begin work on *London in the Nineteenth Century*, a sequel to *Metropolitan Improvements* covering the earlier buildings and antiquities of the capital. During the late summer he also visited Ireland to make sketches for a volume on Dublin which was never published. *Modern Athens* began to appear early in 1829, and *Bath and Bristol . . . displayed . . .*, the only one of the series not to appear in parts, was published later in the year. The last number of *Metropolitan Improvements* and the first number of *London in the Nineteenth Century* came out concurrently in January 1830; the 193 drawings for the latter occupied Thomas Hosmer until well into 1831, while *Modern Athens* was completed in 1830. Thus over a period of five years Thomas Hosmer illustrated four topographical works containing over 450 plates; for each of these he made one or more sketches on the spot, and then prepared in the studio a wash drawing from which the engraver worked.

On 13 September 1828, during his visit to Dublin, Thomas Hosmer issued a prospectus[18] to subscribers to *Metropolitan Improvements* stating his intention of continuing the series with volumes on Edinburgh, Dublin, the English Universities and other cities, sea-ports and watering places. Three months later a further advertisement announced:

Jones's Great Britain Illustrated, in Quarto Numbers, Price One Shilling, each containing 4 Brilliant Steel Engravings by Mr. Thos. H. Shepherd.

Plans for the new volumes appear to have gone ahead, and Thomas Hosmer may have begun to feel a need for assistance, since on 19 December 1829 he advertised for a pupil.[18] Why this project never developed after *Modern Athens* is not clear. Jones and Co. may have run into difficulties, or possibly the five years of intense activity may have begun to tell on Thomas Hosmer. Had he gone on to carry out Jones' grand design, we might well have been deprived of the hundreds of late drawings in which he recorded the unfashionable and obscure side of London. In 1831 and 1832 he showed four Scottish landscapes, presumably sketched while he was engaged on *Modern Athens*, at the Society of British Artists. These are the only occasions on which he is known to have exhibited—he was evidently trying new paths.

Although it had virtually come to an end, Thomas Hosmer's work for Jones and Co. continued to pay him considerable dividends. It had made him well-known and gained him further commissions, which must have been welcome since he now had four children—Frederick Napoleon, Jane Maria, Emma Caroline and the young Thomas Hosmer.[19] The largest was for Partington's somewhat hackneyed compilation *National History and views of London . . .* (1835), for which he supplied nearly 400 drawings, most of them tiny and based on his earlier work. In 1837 a wood-engraving from one of Thomas Hosmer's drawings (pl. 29) appeared in the *Penny Magazine*, probably by no means his only contribution to the new illustrated journalism. In 1840 he began a new group of drawings, interior views of various well-known London institutions. *London Interiors* was published in two series in 1841–44; the first series is largely based on Thomas Hosmer's work, but he does not figure in the second. About 1842 the Shepherd family moved from 26 Chapman Street, by now far too small for them, to 2 Bird's Buildings, [15] now part of Colebrooke Row, just east of Essex Road and close to Camden Passage. This house also survives, an older eighteenth-century building, larger but with less light and air, hemmed in by the early Victorian terraces of east Islington.

Meanwhile George Sidney's career had been developing along rather different lines. In about 1831 he married,[20] and by January 1832 had moved into 20 St Paul's Terrace, Camden Town, an elegant house looking eastwards across the still open fields uphill towards Belle Isle and Islington. This was an ideal situation, midway between Hampstead where he often worked and the West End, and close to picturesque spots like Randall's tile kilns of which he made several studies (pl. 49). During the 1830's George Sidney tried hard to establish himself as a painter, exhibiting at the Academy, the Society of British Artists and the New Society of Painters in Watercolours. His contributions included still lifes and genre subjects as well as townscapes and landscapes, the latter ranging widely over England, Wales, Scotland and the Channel Islands. It is not hard to see why he did not succeed; his work is attractive but not compelling and he did not turn into one of those purveyors of landscapes who made a good living in high Victorian times. He had great ambitions, but lacked the ability and imagination to realise them.

The minutes of the New Society of Painters in Watercolours[21] provide an illuminating commentary on the course of George Sidney's later career. He was one of ten members who met in July 1834 to remodel the Society and set it on a firm footing, and was elected to the provisional committee, but was not included in the managing committee which replaced it in January 1835 (chosen by lot). At about this time he and his family moved from St Paul's Terrace to more confined surroundings at 47 Burton Street, close to Euston Square. George Sidney continued to figure in the Society's minutes, proposing the election of the marine painter Edward Duncan and seconding that of William Haghe. Late in 1836 the Shepherds left Burton Street for 15 Chad's Row, Gray's Inn Road,[22] and early in 1839 moved from there to 14 Charles (Mortimer) Street near the Middlesex Hospital, in each case leaving arrears of rates. Whereas up to 1839 he had sent a number of works to the Society's annual exhibitions at Exeter Hall, in 1840 George Sidney contributed only one, *Lowestoft Lighthouse*, possibly the painting of the same name which he had already shown at the Society of British Artists in 1835.

By the autumn of 1840 he had begun to incur fines for non-attendance at meetings, while already owing the Society money for sales through their exhibitions. Early in 1841 the committee agreed to let him have his frames back, on condition that he used them to submit works to the next exhibition. He sent four works that year, and continued to submit a few to every show during the 1840s, except in 1845. The 1847 catalogue gives George Sidney's address as 154 Balicourt Place, St John Street Road, which has resisted identification. By the summer of 1849 he had moved to 18 Albion (now Balfe) Street, an unattractive place off the southern end of the Caledonian Road. In 1850 George Sidney did not exhibit, perhaps because he was now busy with a series of London views commissioned by Rudolph Ackermann the younger; these were issued in 1851 to coincide with the opening of the Great Exhibition. At about the same time George Sidney moved to 40 Upper Seymour (now Eversholt) Street, Somers Town, close to where he had lived in his youth but now utterly transformed by the coming of the railway. He was now a widower, with a household consisting of his 18 year old unemployed son Percy, Stanfield who was 16 and his father's pupil and 13 year old Fanny who kept house.[7]

George Sidney continued to exhibit with the Society, sending works each year from 1851 to 1858, 22 of them altogether, priced at an average of nine guineas. He ceased however to attend their monthly meetings, probably through ill health. In 1859 he no longer appears in the list of members, and the Society's minutes for 5 November 1860 explain why:

Mr Shepherd's son having made an appeal to the Society on the part of his Father, who is bed-ridden and in great distress . . . and as it appeared that several of the Members had recently given him various sums, it was considered better to give him small sums weekly . . . Mr McKewan and Mr Chase having consented to be the Society's Almoners in this case, it was resolved that . . . a sum of ten pounds be placed in their hands . . . to dispense at their discretion.

On 3 February 1861 a further five pounds was made available. And there George Sidney disappears from view; even his death is unrecorded.

Thomas Hosmer and his family might have starved too, had it not been for the friendship and patronage of Frederick Crace (1779–1859). Crace, a celebrated interior decorator whose greatest achievement was the interior of the Brighton Pavilion, had begun to collect maps and views of London about 1818.[23] His superb collection, now in the British Museum, contains many hundreds of pencil and watercolour drawings by Thomas Hosmer, covering the entire span of his career from 1809 to 1859. It seems to have been in 1844 that Crace began to commission drawings for his collection from Thomas Hosmer, usually of streets and buildings which through his work as a Commissioner of Sewers Crace knew were about to be radically altered or swept away. However, their acquaintance may have begun years before, since Crace obtained for his collection many of Thomas Hosmer's earlier drawings.

Although Crace's support kept Thomas Hosmer and his family from want, they were not immune from personal sorrow. During 1848 Thomas Hosmer apparently did no work at all; this is most unlike him and may well have been a reaction to the illness and death from tuberculosis of two of his grown up children, Thomas Hosmer by then 21 and a trained wood engraver and Emma Caroline.

His eldest son Frederick may have been another source of anxiety to Thomas Hosmer. Born in 1819, by the late 1830's he had developed into quite a promising artist; plate 30 is a good example of his strong, vigorously tinted drawings, characteristically centred on a group of figures. But in about 1840 a catastrophic change took place: his style regressed, became faltering and juvenile, and he even descended to imitating his father's work and attempting to reproduce his signature. Thomas Hosmer's writing on many of Frederick's drawings of this period shows that he tried to help his son through his difficulties. In 1851 Frederick was still living with his parents and is described as a draughtsman on wood;[5] for him, as for his younger brothers Thomas Hosmer and Valentine Claude, wood engraving at least offered a reasonably certain livelihood.

In the early 1850's Thomas Hosmer received the last major commission of his career, for sixteen drawings to illustrate *Mighty London*, published by Read and Co. in 1854. He based most of these on earlier work, although fashions and vehicles acknowledge the world of the 1850s. On 14 July 1851, when London was thronged with visitors to the Great Exhibition, Thomas Hosmer's eldest daughter Jane Maria, aged 30, a schoolmistress, died from an abdominal tumour, and it may have been this which prompted the family to leave Bird's Buildings with its sad associations and move back to the Barnsbury area, to 13 Brunswick (later Reid) Street,[24] a house which no longer exists but which must have been very similar to 26 Chapman Street.

Thomas Hosmer now began to produce drawings at a rate even greater than during his period of intensive activity 25 years earlier. Approximately three-quarters of his 1500 London drawings were made between 1851 and 1859. Many are copies of earlier work, but a good number were freshly drawn; here and there a note reminds one that Thomas Hosmer was growing old: he endorsed a drawing of the Princess Theatre, Oxford Street,[25] made on 17 December 1855, 'hard frost and *wind*'. There was a considerable demand for his drawings which often resulted in his producing three or four copies, the most careful of which is usually that in the Crace Collection. His connection with Crace must if anything have been closer than ever; the latter was now very old and perhaps inclined to spend more time on his collection. Thomas Hosmer certainly visited Crace's home in Hammersmith in the summers of 1854 and 1855,[26] and notes in his hand on the mounts of the Crace Collection suggest that he and Crace may have worked on it together. Their remarkable knowledge of London and of the way in which it had changed during their lifetimes gave them much in common.

Crace died on 18 September 1859, and it is probably not a coincidence that Thomas Hosmer's last dated drawing was produced just five weeks earlier, on 12 August. Although other younger collectors, notably John Edmund Gardner, had been purchasing his work, the death of Crace seems to have marked the end of Thomas Hosmer's long career. He lived on for another five years, dying in Islington at the age of 71 on 4 July 1864.[27]

This was not quite the end of the story. In 1871 Frederick, of whose life during the previous twenty years almost nothing is known, suddenly began a new series of topographical drawings, all apparently commissioned by J. E. Gardner. This must have been an act of charity on the latter's part, since the drawings are a feeble travesty of the Shepherd tradition, in which a basic weakness in perspective is offset by the relatively effective rendering of the picturesque figures which Frederick loved. On the back of one of them, a shaky sketch of St John Street, Clerkenwell,[28] Gardner wrote: '. . . This was the last sketch Shepherd was enabled to take prior to his last and fatal ilness [sic]. 1876.' Frederick seems never to have married; his younger brother Valentine Claude, also an artist and wood engraver, who married in 1866 and died in 1888, was survived only by daughters. With no one to carry on their name or tradition, the Shepherd family passed into almost total oblivion;[29] only the enduring appeal of their work has kept their name alive.

The Shepherd Family

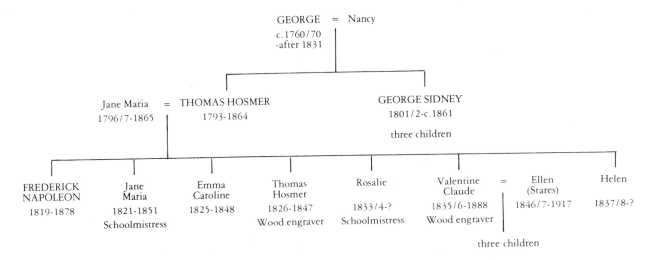

Lombard Street, looking east

PLATE I

Lombard Street appears uncharacteristically deserted in George's robust watercolour of 1810. Of the few passers-by only the errand boy is in haste; an apple woman waits patiently for custom in the massive shadow of St Mary Woolnoth. Contemporary writers often remarked how oddly the workaday, almost drab exterior of Lombard Street contrasted with the importance of the business transacted there.

> After three o'clock p.m. miserable oil lamps tried to enliven the foggy street with their ineffectual light, while through dingy, greenish squares of glass you might observe tall tallow candles dimly disclosing the mysteries of bank or counting-house

wrote Aleph (William Harvey) in the *City Press*. He could almost have been describing the nearest building in the picture, number 76, which housed the old-established bankers Willis, Percival and Co. Later in the day the street would have been crowded with hurrying clerks and departing mail-coaches, since the main post office for the United Kingdom and the colonies was situated there.

Lombard Street had been a centre of financial activity since the later Middle Ages, when an influx of Italian goldsmiths had given it its name. In the seventeenth century it saw the evolution of both banking and underwriting in their modern form. The archway just visible down the street led to Pope's Head Alley, named after a well-known tavern which Pepys visited on 27 November 1665:

> . . . Heard of Cocke and found him at the Pope's Head drinking with Temple . . . the goldsmiths do decry the new act, for money to be all brought into the Exchequer, and paid out thence, saying that they will not advance one farthing upon it . . .

This short-lived measure proved only a temporary set-back to the banking business which the goldsmiths of Lombard Street were carrying on alongside their more traditional activities. Samuel Lee's London Directory, published in 1677 from a shop near Pope's Head Alley, includes a list of the goldsmiths who kept running cashes, in other words provided banking facilities, almost all of whom were in Lombard Street.

In 1692 Edward Lloyd moved his coffee house to the corner of Abchurch Lane, just beyond St Mary Woolnoth. It had already become a favourite meeting place of merchants and shipowners for the transaction of mercantile business, in particular the insurance of vessels and their cargoes. In 1696 Lloyd founded *Lloyd's News* to give his customers a better information service, and by 1700 Lloyd's was widely recognized as an underwriting centre. In 1770 both name and publication were taken over by a formal association of underwriters who set up the institution that we know today, initially in temporary premises in Pope's Head Alley.

Guildhall Library; 353 × 244 mm

The Fleet Prison

PLATE 2

This is one of George's most memorable watercolours. The everyday details of life outside—the cheerful porters, the untidy baskets, the portly official—emphasize the unyielding face of the prison. And yet, as prisons went, the Fleet did not bear a gloomy reputation. Life within its walls was organised to make the experience of confinement for debt as painless as possible. It even possessed an official address, 9 Fleet Market, the number visible in George's drawing, which inmates could use in correspondence without revealing the true facts of their situation.

Once a debtor had obtained his *habeas*, which allowed him to choose his prison, he was more likely to select the Fleet than the other two prisons used mainly for debtors, the King's Bench and the Marshalsea. With sufficient means it was possible to lead a comfortable, even sheltered life there, where, according to the anonymous author of *The Humours of the Fleet* (1749):

> *Kept from the Pow'r of doing Good—or Harm,*
> *Relenting Captives only ruminate*
> *Misconduct past, and curse their present State;*
> *Tho' sorely griev'd, few are so void of Grace,*
> *As not to wear a seeming chearful Face. . . .*

Behind the 35-foot wall lay an irregularly-shaped enclosure, spanned by the main building of the prison which was plain yet almost elegant. Its four floors and basement contained, besides the usual offices and some hundred rooms for the accommodation of paying prisoners, a coffee room, billiard room and a tap-room from which the gaoler derived a considerable income. It is hardly surprising that the threatened destruction of the prison during the Gordon Riots of 1780 caused panic among the inmates, as described in a contemporary account:

About one o'clock this morning (Tuesday, June 6) the Mob went to the Fleet Prison, and demanded the gates to be opened . . . They were then proceeding to demolish the prison, but the prisoners expostulating with them, and begging that they would give them time to remove their goods, they readily condescended, and gave them a day for that purpose, in consequence of which, the prisoners were removing all this day out of that place . . .

Life was harder for the small minority of really destitute prisoners. They sat behind the grille in the wall shown in George's drawing, droning out the monotonous plea: '*Pray* remember the poor prisoners having no allowance'. The money received and the broken victuals deposited in the baskets alongside the grille went towards their maintenance.

The Fleet was finally closed in 1842, when the remaining prisoners were unwillingly transferred to the less congenial surroundings of the Queen's Bench Prison in Southwark, and the site was cleared in 1845–6. It lay just north of Ludgate Circus, on what is now the east side of Farringdon Street.

Greater London Council Print Collection; 181 × 243 mm

Drury Lane Theatre after the fire, 1809

PLATE 3

Late on the evening of 24 February 1809 a brilliant glow spread across London, bringing those who were still awake to windows and rooftops. There was no mistaking its source—Drury Lane Theatre rose head and shoulders above surrounding buildings. Parliament was still sitting, and Sheridan, proprietor of the theatre, hurried from the House to see if anything could be done. It was hopeless: the fire had gained a firm hold and the roof had already fallen in. As the flames roared within the enormous shell, the heat grew tremendous, and the fire brigades did well to save the adjoining houses. Sheridan sat drinking port in a nearby coffee-house, remarking to an anxious friend: "It is hard if a man cannot drink a glass of wine by his own fire".

The third Drury Lane Theatre designed by Henry Holland and opened on 12 March 1794, was an ambitious structure. Ironically, it incorporated elaborate precautions against fire; Holland fitted an iron safety curtain and four large reservoirs at roof level, as well as using iron 'fire plates' in place of more combustible materials. He intended his new theatre to be the centre of a splendid island block containing houses, shops and restaurants, but these were never built, hence the temporary air of the tunnel entrance from Brydges Street and the shoddy board fence covered with old posters.

Although its ashes were still warm, in George's drawing the towering ruin seems as timeless as the Baths of Diocletian.

British Museum: Department of Prints and Drawings (Crace Collection); 243 × 345 mm

St Luke's, Old Street from the north-west

PLATE 4

This early drawing by Thomas Hosmer is a return to the scenes of his childhood. It exactly conveys the character of the unplanned though undeniably picturesque suburban sprawl in which he grew up; Ratcliff Row is just out of sight to the left. Sandwiched between the courts and terraces around the church lay a variety of business premises, among them a rope walk, dye works and a large cooperage. The latter was one of several supplying barrels to the many local breweries, to one of which probably belonged the chimneys glimpsed on the other side of Old Street. The market gardens in the foreground, apparently planted with soft fruit, perhaps gooseberries, not long after became the site of a properly planned development, King Square.

British Museum: Department of Prints and Drawings (Crace Collection); 127 × 188 mm

Bucklersbury

PLATE 5

Until the laying-out of Queen Victoria Street in 1871 obliterated a third of it and divested the remainder of most of its charm, Bucklersbury, running from the back of the Mansion House to Cheapside, was one of the more secretive of City streets. Its north-western end, shown in George's watercolour of *c.* 1809, still sidles characteristically into Cheapside although few if any of the houses shown here survive.

From the sixteenth century onwards Bucklersbury was identified in the minds of Londoners with the fragrance and mystery of the apothecary. Stow states categorically in his *Survey of London* that 'this whole street, on both the sides thereof, is possessed of grocers and apothecaries'. In his bluff wooing of Mistress Ford, Falstaff declares,

Come, I cannot cog and say thou art this and that, like a many of these lisping hawthorn buds, that come like women in men's apparel and smell like Bucklersbury in simple-time: I cannot; but I love thee, none but thee, and thou deservest it.

In more serious vein, Sir Thomas Browne observes in *Religio Medici*: "I know most of the plants of my country, and of those about me, yet methinks I do not know so many as when I did but know a hundred and had scarcely ever simpled further than Cheapside". By the beginning of the nineteenth century the street had lost its distinctive character. Only a few druggists remained, the remainder having been replaced by a mixed population of solicitors, bankers, merchants and bill-brokers. In both this drawing and George's view of Lombard Street, the extensive provision of oil street lamps is striking. The woman carrying pails of milk has just come from one of the numerous dairies in which cows were kept in the very heart of the city (see pl. 30). She is unlikely to be a milk-seller, since the weight of milk made this a predominantly male occupation.

Greater London Council Print Collection; 287 × 191 mm

The Old Bailey

PLATE 6

The Sessions House and Newgate Prison, both designed by George Dance, dominate Thomas Hosmer's 1814 aquatint. Dickens expressed the feeling they inspired when he described the Prison's majestic portals as 'looking as if they were made for the express purpose of letting people in, and never letting them out again' (*Sketches by Boz*, 1836). Little more than a year before Thomas Hosmer drew it, Elizabeth Fry had visited the Prison for the first time. Although the new building, completed in 1783, had to some extent remedied the defects of its predecessor, conditions there were still very bad. This was particularly true of the female side, where 300 women and their children were herded together with little food, bedding or sanitation. In spite of fears for their safety, Mrs Fry and her companions insisted on going in among the women. Their calm concern and obvious sincerity disarmed the normally violent and abusive inmates—"I heard weeping, and I thought they appeared very much tendered", she wrote. In 1897 her newly-formed Ladies' Prison Visiting Association began work in earnest. Their success in transforming the atmosphere of the place gradually forced the authorities to recognize what could be done.

From 1783 onwards public executions were held in the street in front of the prison instead of at Tyburn. Among those who suffered here were Bellingham, the half-crazed assassin of the Prime Minister Spencer Perceval, Thistlewood and the other Cato Street Conspirators, and the banker Henry Fauntleroy, perpetrator of an enormous fraud. Forgery was one of the commonest capital offences; early one morning in the 1820's the artist George Cruikshank, a contemporary of Thomas Hosmer, saw two women hanged here for passing forged £1 notes, of which there were a number in circulation. This so appalled him that he immediately designed a grim parody of a £1 note, adorned with symbols of the scaffold and signed 'J. Ketch'. It was published by the radical bookseller and pamphleteer William Hone, whose shop was in Old Bailey almost opposite the Prison. The directors of the Bank of England were incensed, but the notes sold like hot cakes and achieved their aim: never again was anyone hanged for passing forged notes.

The print illustrated is of particular interest, since it is an outline etching which the artist has touched up, coloured and signed to indicate that it is the definitive version of the subject, upon which his final application of aquatint ground and the hand-colouring of the finished plates were to be based (see *Guide to London drawings*, p. 104).

Greater London Council Print Collection; 178 × 122 mm

COMMON STAGE WAGGON TO R

T.H. Shepherd 18

Coade and Sealy's Artificial Stone Manufactory

PLATE 7

By 1800 wharves and factories lined the South Bank north of Westminster Bridge. Behind Martineau's brewery lay these workshops, from which came much of the architectural ornament of Georgian London. Coade's 1784 catalogue lists 788 items, ranging from John Bacon's famous River God costing £105, of which George shows a specimen, to simple balusters at six shillings each. Made from kaolin mixed with finely-ground quartz or glass and carefully fired, Coade stone appears to last almost indefinitely. The best-known example is the lion now installed at the east end of Westminster Bridge, but scores of elegant keystones can still be seen in Bedford Square or Harley Street.

George's watercolour of c. 1810–15 is unsigned—most unusual for him.

Guildhall Library; 217 × 289 mm

The Royal Exchange

PLATE 8

There are few better examples than this drawing of the young Thomas Hosmer's outstanding ability in drawing architecture, although only two-thirds of it can be shown here. His eye for detail, assured perspective and unerring sense of design together produce an overwhelming impression of *solidity*. This drawing, probably made during the first half of 1816, was worked up by Havell into an aquatint published by Ackermann on 1 July. In spite of his great experience, Havell was unable to avoid substituting Cockney caricature for the delicate anonymity of Thomas Hosmer's figures.

The Cornhill front, shown here, was the principal façade of the second Royal Exchange, designed by the City surveyor Edward Jarman to replace Sir Thomas Gresham's original building which was destroyed in the Great Fire. Jarman's attempt to create an imposing entrance is slightly absurd in its earnest piling of Pelion upon Ossa, but its busy detail, meticulously recorded by Thomas Hosmer, must have endeared it to generations of City men. Above the twin shops, offering appropriately enough newspapers and medicines, are heroic statues of Charles I and Charles II; higher up, busts of Queen Elizabeth crown the balustrades and clock-tower, which is surmounted by a grasshopper weathervane— the Gresham crest. The apparent massiveness of Jarman's edifice was deceptive. The clock-tower was in fact of timber, and badly in need of repair; in 1821 it had to be taken down, together with much of the entrance, and a sympathetically designed replacement constructed. The Royal Exchange must have been a popular subject, since in 1836 Ackermann brought out a second edition of their 1816 aquatint for which Havell's original plate was carefully altered to show the new tower. One hopes that the edition sold out quickly, before the burning of the Exchange on 10 January 1838 made it out of date again.

As always, Thomas Hosmer provides a well-orchestrated street scene to offset the architecture. The coach is setting off via Aldgate and Mile End to some destination in East Anglia. The turbanned figures glimpsed between the shops bring to mind Addison's famous reflection on the Exchange[30] a century earlier, even more true in 1816:

There is no place in the town which I so much love to frequent as the Royal Exchange. It gives me a secret satisfaction, and in some measure gratifies my vanity, as I am an Englishman, to see so rich an assembly of countrymen and foreigners consulting together upon the private business of mankind, and making this metropolis a kind of emporium for the whole earth. I must confess I look upon High 'Change to be a great council in which all considerable nations have their representatives. . . . I have often been pleased to hear disputes adjusted between an inhabitant of Japan and an alderman of London; or to see a subject of the great Mogul entering into a league with one of the Czar of Muscovy. . . . Sometimes I am jostled among a body of Armenians; sometimes I am lost in a crowd of Jews; and sometimes make one in a group of Dutchmen. I am a Dane, Swede, or Frenchman at different times; or rather, fancy myself like the old philosopher, who, upon being asked what countryman he was replied that he was a citizen of the world.

British Museum: Department of Prints and Drawings (Crace Collection); 386 × 479 mm

The Bull and Mouth Inn

PLATE 9

The *Bull and Mouth* acquired its strange name in the same way as the *Elephant and Castle*, by corruption. But whereas the castle at least formed part of the arms of the *Infanta of Castille*, the *Boulogne Mouth* had no connection with bulls or mouths: it was named after the harbour of Boulogne, captured by Henry VIII in 1544. The inn was burnt in the Great Fire, but rebuilt to a fairly traditional pattern, as George's watercolour of 1817 shows. George's interest was in the architecture, and the stage waggons and the pile of packages waiting to be shifted give no hint that this was in fact one of London's major coaching inns.

For a brief period, little more than half a century, up to about 1840 the mail-coach proprietors and inn-keepers enjoyed a golden age. Besides creating a demand for more efficient freight transport, largely met through the construction of canals, the Industrial Revolution stimulated the growth of passenger traffic between the provinces and London. Improvements in road engineering and construction and more sophisticated organisation along the coach routes made possible much faster travelling. Coach journeys were still very slow; in 1818 it took over a day to travel the 186 miles from London to Manchester.

The *Bull and Mouth* had now become one of the major London starting-points for mail-coaches serving the north and north-west; from it one could leave for many destinations including Edinburgh and Glasgow, Leeds and Nottingham, Birmingham and Shrewsbury, Worcester and Ludlow. Although the operation of mail-coach lines was now a well-organised and often highly profitable business, it was some time before this began to be reflected in the buildings from which it was carried on. The *Bull and Mouth* had no impressive façade to attract attention —in fact it was tucked obscurely away down a narrow turning off St Martin's-le-Grand. The only concession made to passengers was a coffee-room, just out of sight to the left, where they could wait and refresh themselves.

In 1823 Edward Sherman, one of the most enterprising of the coach operators, established himself at the *Bull and Mouth*. He soon introduced coaches which by starting at an early hour reached Manchester the same day, and set up a *Bull and Mouth* coach office at Piccadilly Circus to serve westbound routes. The old buildings off St Martin's-le-Grand soon proved inadequate, and in 1828 Sherman obtained a new lease from the ground landlord, Christ's Hospital, and rebuilt the *Bull and Mouth* as the *Queen's Hotel*. The new building, opened in 1830, occupied a larger site, with an imposing entrance front on St Martin's-le-Grand directly opposite the recently-erected General Post Office. It was now the terminus of an extensive service: on Mondays 21 coaches left for the north-west and 21 travelled from there to London.

The great days of the *Queen's Hotel* lasted only a few years, but it survived the advent of railways and the decline of the coaching business. Although not near any of the railway termini it was well situated close to the heart of the City, and remained a favourite stopping-place for Manchester men. It was eventually demolished in 1887 to make way for Post Office premises.

Guildhall Library; 278 × 201 mm

Hungerford Stairs

PLATE 10

When in 1814 George Shepherd took his sketching pad to Hungerford Stairs at low tide, and looked back towards the spire of St Martin-in-the-Fields, the scene had changed very little in a hundred years. In 1682 Sir Edward Hungerford had founded a market here as a rival to Covent Garden. Not a success, it hung on in slow decay throughout the eighteenth century. As he drew, George had no inkling of the important role which the shabby *Old Fox*, in shadow on the right, would shortly play in the formation of one of England's greatest writers. By the 1820s it had become, as 80 Hungerford Stairs, the warehouse of Jonathan Warren's blacking business. The parents of Charles Dickens sent him to drudge there for six shillings a week at the age of 10.

The blacking warehouse was the last house on the left-hand side of the way at old Hungerford Stairs. It was a crazy, break-down old house, abutting on the river, of course, and literally over-run with rats. Its wainscoted rooms, its rotten floors and staircases, and the old grey rats swarming down in the cellars and coming up the stairs at all times, and the dirt and decay of the place, rise up visibly before me, as if I were there again. The counting house was on the first floor, looking over the coal-barges and the river. There was in it a recess where I used to sit and work. My work was to cover the pots of paste-blacking first with a piece of oil-paper, and then with a piece of blue-paper, to tie them round with string, and then to clip the paper close to them making it neat all round until it looked as smart as a pot of ointment from an apothecary's shop. When a certain number of grosses of pots had attained this pitch of perfection I was to paste on each a printed label, and then go on again with more pots.

Dickens used this experience, with some variations and different names, in *David Copperfield*. The whole area was cleared in about 1830 for the construction of the new Hungerford Market.

Greater London Council Print Collection; 223 × 143 mm

Clare Market

PLATE 11

Founded by the Earl of Clare in 1657, this was the first of London's local markets, soon to be followed by Hungerford Market, Newport Market and others. Held twice a week, Strype described it as 'very considerable and well served with provisions, both flesh and fish; for besides the butchers in the shambles, it is much resorted to by the country butchers and higglers' (egg-sellers). By the early nineteenth century the area had gone down in the world, and the market with it; rows of wooden stalls, selling vegetables as well as meat, had attached themselves to Lord Clare's original seventeenth-century market house.

The posters in the foreground reflect some of the preoccupations of Londoners in June 1815—the high price of bread, the annual state lottery and the Shakespearean triumphs of Edmund Kean. The Corn Bill against which a petition had been organised had in fact become law in March; it attempted to protect British agriculture by prohibiting the importation of corn until the price of home-grown wheat had risen to the high level of 80 shillings a quarter, and was expected to lead to even higher bread prices. An annual lottery was a feature of Government finance until Victorian times—this one was launched the day before George made the drawing. After a long apprenticeship in the provinces, Edmund Kean had begun his spectacular career at the nearby Drury Lane Theatre early in the previous year; the poster advertises *Othello*, one of his best-known roles. The last poster is a punning adaptation of a standard theatre 'benefit night' poster on which George has inserted his own name and the date—8 June 1815.

Guildhall Library; 235 × 220 mm

The Strand

PLATE 12

The great Aldwych-Kingsway scheme, which transformed the eastern half of the Strand at the beginning of the century, cleared slums and improved communications at the cost of a devastating change in scale. Until then, St Mary-le-Strand on its island site and the mighty front of Somerset House had provided the main focal points. Now the church is dwarfed by the sub-classical bulk of Bush House, against which even Somerset House can barely hold its own.

St Mary-le-Strand was one of the fifty new churches, of which only a handful were built, intended as a thank-offering for the ending of the War of the Spanish Succession. Its design was the first commission received by James Gibbs on his return from Rome, and reflects what he had learnt there. The exception is the steeple, rising from the westernmost bay in a manner recalling his more famous church of St Martin-in-the-Fields. The original intention was to provide a small campanile only, with 80 feet to the west a free-standing column crowned by a statue of Queen Anne. This was abandoned in favour of the slender steeple.

Shoddy workmanship at the time of the church's construction led to a tragedy 80 years later, in 1802. The short-lived Peace of Amiens was about to be proclaimed, and crowds lined the Strand to watch the heralds ride to the Royal Exchange. A man standing on the roof of St Mary-le-Strand pressed against one of the elegant urns along the balustrade, which fell without warning into the densely-packed street below, killing or injuring several people. When examined, the urn was found to have been attached by a wooden spike instead of an iron clamp.

Like plate 6, this is an outline etching, a preliminary stage in the preparation of an aquatint, involving both artist and engraver. After etching the outline of Thomas Hosmer's drawing on the plate, the engraver J. Bluck ran off a few proof copies, one of which Thomas Hosmer coloured and touched up by hand to guide Bluck and the colourists in their final preparation of the aquatint, published by Ackermann in January 1819. Bluck took unusual pains to render Thomas Hosmer's animated street scenes, of which this is another fine example. It represents an entire cross-section of society. On the extreme left a porter moves steadily Citywards, passed by an aristocratic carriage heading for the West End. The four troopers, light dragoons, are riding at ease, sabres drawn to salute any officer they meet; they could easily be veterans of Waterloo. The little figure with ladder and oil-can is a lamp-lighter; one had to be active to replenish all the lamps during the short days of winter, hence the phrase *going like a lamplighter*. The drover and his sheep are nearing Smithfield.

The man standing almost in the path of the stage-coach is holding a placard, on which the name TURNER is just legible. J. M. W. Turner is not known to have mounted a one-man exhibition during the autumn of 1818, but it reminds us of the fact that from 1780 until 1837 the rooms of the Royal Academy were in the right-hand side of the Strand front of Somerset House, shown on the portion of the outline etching not reproduced here, which forms the front of the dust-jacket.

Museum of London; 343 × 483 mm

The Banqueting House, Whitehall

PLATE 13

At first sight this drawing is perplexing. It unmistakably represents Inigo Jones's Banqueting House in Whitehall, but also includes the 'Holbein' Gate and other parts of the old Palace of Whitehall which had disappeared long before 1821 when Thomas Hosmer made the drawing. The antiquated sedan chairs and hackney coaches strike a further anachronistic note. The explanation is fairly simple. It was drawn for the topographical publisher Joseph Mawman, who in 1821 brought out an English translation of the *Travels of Cosmo the Third, Grand Duke of Tuscany, through England. . . . (1669)*. To illustrate it an unknown artist copied the 39 contemporary drawings accompanying the original manuscript in the Laurentian Library, Florence. Thomas Hosmer was given the somewhat thankless task of redrawing these large, coarse copies at a much smaller size for aquatinting.[31] He achieved this so skilfully, without alteration or loss of detail, that their quality is sharpened and their period flavour enhanced.

Each of the Shepherds produced anachronistic drawings at some stage in his career, either direct copies of earlier drawings or engravings or imaginative reconstructions of their own. George made copies for Wilkinson's *Londina Illustrata* from various sources, drawing particularly on Hollar's 1647 panorama of London. George Sidney amused himself with a few rather unconvincing period views, and Frederick did a good many—they allowed him to indulge his taste for outlandish figures and dress.

British Museum: Department of Prints and Drawings (Crace Collection); 152 × 262 mm

Smithfield Market, 1824

PLATE 14

It was market morning. . . . A thick steam perpetually rising from the reeking bodies of the cattle . . . hung heavily above. All the pens in the centre of the large area, and as many temporary pens as could be crowded into the vacant space, were filled with sheep; tied up to posts by the gutter side were long lines of beasts and oxen, three or four deep. Countrymen, butchers, drovers, hawkers, boys, thieves, idlers and vagabonds of every low grade, were mingled together in a mass; the whistling of drovers, the barking of dogs, the bellowing and plunging of oxen, the bleating of sheep, the grunting and squeaking of pigs, the cries of hawkers, the shouts, oaths, and quarrelling on all sides; the ringing of bells and roar of voices, that issued from every public house; the crowding, pushing, driving, beating, whooping and yelling; the hideous and discordant din that resounded from every corner of the market; and the unwashed, unshaven, squalid and dirty figures constantly running to and fro, and bursting in and out of the throng; rendered it a stunning and bewildering scene, which quite confounded the senses.

Dickens' description of Smithfield in *Oliver Twist* finds a remarkably close parallel in George Sidney's 'sketch for a Large Picture', drawn about the time that the young Dickens was beginning to acquire his unique knowledge of London. The 'Large Picture' does not seem to have survived—if it was ever painted—and might well have lacked the vigour and immediacy of this drawing. We are looking across the market from the corner of the appropriately-named Cow Lane at the eighteenth-century gateway of Bart's and the dome of St Paul's, hazy in the heat rising from the milling throng of men and animals. In the foreground a street-seller with her tray of food is picking her way past tethered cattle and flocks of sheep. George Sidney has effectively captured the bustle of a crowd, something which neither George nor Thomas Hosmer ever attempted, and one wonders if he did more work in this vein.

Guildhall Library; 211 × 283 mm

Regent Circus

PLATE 15

Thomas Hosmer's original drawing for this 1822 aquatint, also in the Crace Collection, is, sadly, too faint for reproduction. It is a minor masterpiece, in which he succeeds in evoking the fashionable bustle of what we now call Piccadilly Circus while endowing the numerous figures peopling it with carefully-observed, even eccentric individuality. This was evidently more than Ackermann had bargained for, and the aquatint is a toned-down version, omitting the less conventional figures, to which the Bath coach hastening towards the Golden Cross now adds a vital touch of panache.

Even with its detail diluted this view remains topographically most effective. It shows how Lower Regent Street was aligned on Carlton House, with behind it, and perhaps shown a little too prominently, Westminster Hall and the tower of St Margaret's. The rows of elegant lampstandards are a reminder of the fact that by 1822 gas street lighting was becoming quite common in the West End.

British Museum; Department of Prints and Drawings (Crace Collection); 344 × 492 mm

The Vale of Health

PLATE 16

The Vale of Health has not always been regarded as one of the pleasantest corners of Hampstead. Mrs Nollekens, the wife of the sculptor, is said to have called it 'a stagnate bottom, a pit in the Heath . . .', a fair description of what was then a marshy spot called Hatches Bottom. In 1777 London's increasing demand for water led the Hampstead Water Company to form the pond which still exists on the east side of the Vale. This had the effect of draining the area, and by 1780 a number of modest houses had been built.

In the early nineteenth century the Vale of Health's most famous resident was Leigh Hunt, the writer and editor, who lived there from 1815 to 1819 and again in 1820–21. Keats first called on him on 1 December 1816, and during his frequent visits over the next two years met Shelley and many other literary men there. George's 1825 drawing captures the charm of the place very successfully, but the gypsies added to give interest to the foreground seem rather unconvincing against the confident pencil and wash work behind.

Victoria and Albert Museum: Department of Prints and Drawings; 254 × 343 mm

The City Basin, Regent's Canal

PLATE 17

When the Grand Junction Canal was completed in 1801 the London area was for the first time linked with the great waterway system of the industrial Midlands and North, and the Paddington Basin soon began to handle a growing tonnage of freight. This coincided with the excavation of the West India Docks, the first of the great docks downriver which were to restore the pre-eminence of the Port of London. Old London Bridge was a barrier to river traffic, and a canal running from Paddington around the north of London to reach the Thames at Limehouse was first proposed as early as 1802. The idea was taken up again in 1811 by John Nash in connection with his plans for the development of Regent's Park, and the canal itself completed after many vicissitudes in 1820.

Its very high cost of construction—over $£\frac{1}{2}$ million for $8\frac{1}{2}$ miles of works, including two tunnels and several intermediate basins—and its late arrival on the scene, only twenty years before railways began to compete seriously for freight, meant that the Regent's Canal was never a paying proposition, but this did not prevent it being much used during the first few years of its existence. Thomas Hosmer's 1825 watercolour shows the City (Road) Basin, which stretched 600 yards southwards from the Canal like a finger pointed at the heart of the City. Its wharves were already lined with warehouses belonging to firms handling a predictable range of merchandise: coal, stone, timber, iron, salt, china and earthenware. In addition there were the great carrying businesses; Snell and Brice, whose barge is making for their wharf at 7 City Basin, and Pickford and Co., whose extensive premises can be glimpsed beyond the bridge carrying the City Road.

Thomas Hosmer drew this watercolour for *A Picturesque Tour on the Regent's Canal* (1825); it is one of his most successful compositions, repeated almost line for line in *Metropolitan Improvements*. The steeple on the horizon is St Luke's, Old Street.

Museum of London; 240 × 365 mm

Canonbury Tower, Islington

PLATE 18

By 1820, when Thomas Hosmer came to live there, Islington had become a suburb. Although still surrounded by fields except on the south, where a narrow band of building around the Angel linked it to London, its population rose between 1811 and 1821 from 15,000 to 22,000, largely as a result of the outward migration of which the Shepherds formed part. Canonbury still retained a rural atmosphere, as this drawing shows; the fence in the background skirted a large pond. But the New North Road had already crossed the fields from Hoxton to pass through Canonbury Square, and there were tea gardens just east of the Tower.

Islington rates three engravings in *London in the Nineteenth Century*, more than any other outlying suburb. One inevitably features Canonbury Tower, its oldest and most interesting building. It was built as a country retreat by Prior Bolton, the last Prior of St Bartholomew's, Smithfield before the Reformation. In the eighteenth century it housed a succession of notable people, including the famous Speaker of the House of Commons, Arthur Onslow, John Newbery, the publisher of children's books, and Oliver Goldsmith.

Greater London Council Print Collection; 103 × 64 mm

St John's, Smith Square

PLATE 19

Thomas Hosmer's preliminary sketches for *Metropolitan Improvements* and *London in the Nineteenth Century* are much rarer than the wash drawings prepared from them for engraving, of which *Canonbury Tower* is a good example. This sketch reveals a good deal about his methods of working. Although there is evidence in the form of surviving tracings to show that, like many other artists, Thomas Hosmer on occasion used a *camera obscura* to establish the outlines of buildings, the corrected perspective to left and right in this sketch shows that he did not do so here. The diagram at the foot is a more symmetrical design rejected in favour of the one adopted. Whether or not Thomas Hosmer observed them in Smith Square or in some other place, the organgrinder and his monkey duly appeared in the foreground when the subject was used for plate 129 of *London in the Nineteenth Century*.

Archives Department, Westminster City Libraries; 124 × 183 mm overall

St Johns westminster, April 22 31

M Archer.
Architect

Bunyan's Meeting House, Gravel Lane, Southwark

PLATE 20

From Puritan times down to the days of C. H. Spurgeon, Southwark played an important part in the history of Protestant nonconformity. Between 1662 and 1688 its alleys gave sanctuary to several hard-pressed congregations during the legal persecution they endured. In 1687 the Baptists of Southwark established a meeting house[32] in a quiet turning off Gravel Lane, later appropriately named Zoar Street after the city in which Lot took refuge. It could have begun life as a barn, to judge from its timber-framed three-bay construction. Bunyan is said to have preached there more than once, but this seems doubtful since he died in 1688. The field in the foreground was one of Southwark's many tenter grounds where cloth was stretched on tenterhooks.

This drawing shows that Thomas Hosmer's mature style was largely formed before he reached 20. His accomplished handling of the subject is in marked contrast to his 1809 drawing;[12] his work can already be distinguished from his father's by its softer outline.

Guildhall Library; 181 × 251 mm

The two smallest houses in Holborn

PLATE 21

One of the best of Thomas Hosmer's late watercolours (c. 1852), this shows the north side of High Holborn. On the right, tall jars in the window of number 27 disclose the trade of John Hooper and Sons, wholesale confectioners. Next door a much older house, possibly going back to the seventeenth century, has recently been taken over by the enterprising Parisian firm of Aimé Boura. Dyeing was in great demand to freshen the appearance of clothes, regularly passed on in large Victorian families—and to turn them black for mourning. Boura may have pioneered the revolutionary dry cleaning process, discovered in 1849 in Paris.

The dark passage between 28 and 30 leads to 29, *The Little Coach and Horses*, whose landlord is Henry Pacy, a widower with seven young children. He may be the figure standing in the doorway of number 30, his lately-acquired jug-and-bottle department. On the extreme left the eyecatching window display of J. F. Timms' newly-founded photographic establishment heralds the new technique which will within a generation largely supersede topographical drawing.

Greater London Council Print Collection; 189 × 236 mm

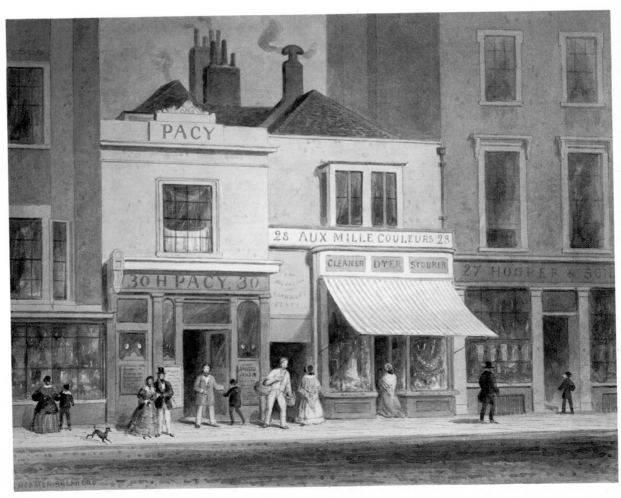

Shepherdess Walk, Islington

PLATE 22

Shepherdess Walk is still recognizably a field path in Frederick's deft little watercolour of 1842; as the shortest route from St Luke's to Islington, it must have been long familiar to the Shepherds. It took its rural-sounding name from the old-established *Shepherd and Shepherdess* tea-gardens at its City Road end, where it also skirted St Luke's Workhouse which was to be Frederick's last home.

Islington Local History Collection; 102 × 146 mm

The last of Bagnigge Wells

PLATE 23

The oddly-named and now almost totally forgotten Bagnigge Wells in its heyday rivalled Sadler's Wells as a popular resort of Londoners. A spring in a field close to the river Fleet, by what was later called King's Cross Road, became the focus of a spa opened to the public in 1759. Bagnigge House with its Long Room adjoined the road; behind them gardens, furnished with seats and arbours, ran along both banks of the Fleet. In these rustic surroundings the waters could be drunk for 3d or taken away at 8d a gallon; the opening announcement stated that 'three half pints of the purging water is sufficient for most people'. Other attractions included feats of strength by the redoubtable Thomas Topham and organ concerts in the Long Room. Lines from Garrick's comedy *Bon Ton* capture the flavour of the place:

> *. . . drinking tea on summer's afternoons*
> *At Bagnigge Wells, with china and gilt spoons*

By 1830 the growth of London had engulfed Bagnigge Wells. Streets and squares now stretched across the fields towards Sadler's Wells; one of the new residents, George Cruikshank, commented on what he saw around him in his famous cartoon *The March of Bricks and Mortar*. The house and gardens finally closed in 1841.

George Sidney's watercolour, dated 2 November 1842 on the mount, shows the Long Room in the last stages of demolition. The chimney towering behind symbolises the forces of change; it belonged to one of the Cubitt brothers' building yards.

Greater London Council Print Collection; 138 × 209 mm

Drury Court

PLATE 24

Drury Court branched southwards from Drury Lane at the point where it now joins the Aldwych; today Bush House covers the site. It escaped the Fire, and the houses in sunlight on the east side of the street date from the seventeenth century or even possibly the late sixteenth century when it is first shown on maps. Until it disappeared in the early 1900s during the clearance for the great Aldwych-Kingsway scheme, Drury Court was a favourite subject for artists, although most drew the north end where it joined Drury Lane, whereas George Sidney gives us the view looking south towards St Mary-le-Strand.

Beneath his signature and the date he has carefully inscribed '*Painted on the spot*'—probably during the summer or early autumn of 1833, to judge from the light clothing of some of the people shown. Reproduction in black and white only partly conveys the strong, truthful colours of this drawing. The greengrocer's vivid display and the barber's sign, the lettering of which stands out on a rich maroon background, contrast with the muted plastering of the houses receding into the misty distance of the Strand. George Sidney has made extensive use of gum arabic to give depth and solidity to the shadows.

The occupations of Drury Court were many and various. Those at the south end nearest the Strand included an undertaker, coffee-house keeper and a bookseller, giving way further up to more modest establishments. At the extreme left in George's Sidney's drawing is P. Longley, plumber and turner, next door a green grocer and beyond that the drab frontage of William Gardiner's glass-silvering business. The sign *Work done by horse and cart* probably marks the premises of William Wells who was mainly a dealer in second-hand furniture. He is perhaps helping the little family group in the foreground to move their furniture and household goods, which almost block the roadway.

Greater London Council Print Collection; 325 × 250 mm

Ruins of the New Brunswick Theatre, 1828

PLATE 25

The Royal Brunswick Theatre opened on Monday, 25 February 1828 with a gala performance attended by 3000 people. There had been a theatre on the site, just north of the London Docks, since 1787, but the new building was larger and more splendid than its predecessor. The first performances were marred by small hitches—the scenery stuck in its grooves and the box doors could not be closed—but their ominous significance was not realised.

Three days after the opening a morning dress rehearsal of *Guy Mannering* was under way, when without warning the entire roof collapsed, carrying with it the elegant façade which fell into Well Street. Twelve people were killed; others had remarkable escapes. The manager, Percy Farren, was watching the rehearsal when a rumble made him look up; a trembling chandelier caught his eye. He leapt into a box, pulling a small girl after him, as the building fell about their ears. When the dust had cleared they found themselves perched precariously on the ruins.

The fall of the theatre was a nine days' wonder. Crowds gathered as rescuers, including workmen from the nearby St Katharine Docks led by their architect Philip Hardwick, delved among the ruins. A crop of crude lithographs and woodcuts of the disaster were rushed out to meet public demand; Thomas Hosmer's sketch is a sober, more detailed record of the scene. Taken from the opposite side of Well Street, it shows the remains of the front wall still blocking the roadway.

Greater London Council Print Collection; 114 × 185 mm

Gloucester Lodge, Regent's Park

PLATE 26

In this late wash drawing of *c.* 1828, George has used the elegant north-eastern entrance to the Park to form a curiously compelling composition. It invites one to pass between the Doric columns and strike out across the as yet largely unplanted expanse of the Park towards the turret of St John's Wood Chapel. I have traced seven of these tiny drawings, the remainder of which are full watercolours; they look as though they were prepared for engraving, but never seem to have been published.

Archives Department, Westminster City Libraries; 60 × 94 mm

Ruins of the New Brunswick Theatre. April 30. 1828 as they appeared immediately after it fell

Geo. Scharf

Charing Cross

PLATE 27

Charing Cross, by which our ancestors meant the three-sided *place* where the Strand, Whitehall and Cockspur Street met, was the hub of the West End long before Piccadilly Circus existed, as Boswell records:

I talked of the cheerfulness of Fleet Street, owing to the quick succession of people which we perceive passing through it.
Johnson. "Why, sir, Fleet Street has a very animated appearance; but I think the full tide of human existence is at Charing Cross."

George Sidney's watercolour shows that even in 1835 some of the bustle remained. Horse buses and carriages pass and repass; a porter and a coachman make their way past elegant sightseers; children longingly eye the streetseller's basket; the sweeper watches over his crossing; a placard presents the current attraction at Burford's Panorama (see pl. 51). At any moment the approaching shower will send them scurrying for shelter.

Although something of the atmosphere survived, in other ways the scene had changed so radically since Johnson's day that only the statue of Charles I would have enabled him to recognise it. Erected in 1675 on the site of the medieval Eleanor Cross which gave the place its name, the statue had a remarkable history. Made in 1633 by the French sculptor Hubert le Sueur for Lord Treasurer Weston, it was intended for his house at Roehampton but was never taken there. It survived the Commonwealth, and after a long legal wrangle over its ownership was placed in its present position, looking towards the site of Charles's execution.

In Johnson's time the famous *Golden Cross Inn* stood directly behind the statue, adjoining the extensive yard of the King's Mews (stables) covering what was later to be Trafalgar Square. The splendour of St Martin-in-the-Fields was completely hidden from view. John Nash perceived the possibilities of this sloping site, and during the 1820's the Square was formed. Besides linking it with Regent Street and his scheme for the West Strand, he planned a direct route northwards to the British Museum, but this was never carried out, and Nash would hardly have approved of the later substitute, Charing Cross Road.

Nash reserved the north side of the Square for the National Gallery, intended to be its dominant feature. As eventually designed it is inadequate for this role, but this is not entirely the fault of the architect, Wilkins, hampered as he was by a limited budget and by being required to re-use the columns and capitals from the recently demolished Carlton House. The terrace in front was intended to increase the impressiveness of its façade, but its effect was cancelled out by the erection of Nelson's Column, completed in 1843. The Gallery was under construction from 1832 until 1838, and is still screened by hoardings in George Sidney's view.

It is hard to realise that until the 1820's James Gibbs' magnificent church, completed in 1726, faced mean houses across a narrow lane. St Martin-in-the-Fields, whose unorthodox combination of portico and tower is repeated many times in the British Isles and in America, is indispensable to what Peel described as 'the finest site in Europe'.

Museum of London; 386 × 287 mm

Geo. Sidney Shepherd. 1835.

Hoare's Bank, Fleet Street

PLATE 28

Hoare's began as goldsmiths in Cheapside, moving to Fleet Street in 1690. The business prospered, and when in 1702 Richard took his son Henry into partnership he described himself as *Banker and Goldsmith*; by the time of his death in 1718 the banking side was becoming dominant. In 1829 Hoare's decided to rebuild their banking house and commissioned a drawing of the old premises from Thomas Hosmer. The result was this superb composition, with its subtle emphasis on number 37, which could almost be described as a portrait of the old building.

One wonders what an old-established and respectable firm like Messrs Hoare can have thought of their new neighbours, the recently-founded but already notorious publication *John Bull*. The dashing cabriolet, a vehicle made popular by Alfred d'Orsay, strikes a modern note, counterbalanced to the right by a corner of the seventeenth-century Gothic St Dunstan's, Fleet Street, itself soon to be rebuilt.

Reproduced by courtesy of Messrs Hoare; 272 × 377 mm

The Zoological Gardens, Regent's Park

PLATE 29

When Thomas Hosmer made this sprightly sketch, on 27 September 1837, the Gardens had been established for nearly ten years. They were intended for scientific research rather than public entertainment, and entry was at first restricted. This was still the case in 1837, to judge from the fashionable appearance of these early Victorians. One hopes that they had seen the notice which read:

LADIES ARE RESPECTFULLY REQUESTED NOT TO TOUCH ANY OF THE ANIMALS WITH THEIR PARASOLS, CONSIDERABLE INJURY HAVING ARISEN FROM THIS PRACTICE

For those unable to visit the Gardens, the *Penny Magazine* for 16 December 1837 contained a wood-engraving based on this drawing.

The view is from the south, looking north-west towards the bare summit of Primrose Hill. On the grass in the foreground are movable aviaries; behind them to the right, half-hidden by trees and ornamental shrubs, appears the conical roof of the Eagles' Aviary, with, in front of it, the Wolf's Den. To the left stands the Llama House, later the Camel House, easily recognized by its clock turret; this building still survives, in a different position. There is no mistaking the Bear Pit.

Guildhall Library; 114 × 187 mm

Zoological Gardens. Regent Park. Sep.r 29.th 1837

Old Hungerford Market

PLATE 30

It seems unlikely that Frederick—born in 1819—drew the old Hungerford Market before it was cleared away about 1830. When he made this drawing, about 1839, he probably relied on his father's sketches, and on the engraving of the Market from a slightly different angle in *London in the Nineteenth Century*. Frederick's rendering of architecture is never more than passable, but there is a vigour and gaiety in his figure drawing here that very largely disappears from his work after 1840 (compare pl. 31). The modest looking shed marked *British Fire Office* housed that insurance company's manually-operated fire-engine, ready to be hurried out into the Strand and away to any fire threatening insured property in the West End.

The new Hungerford Market, opened in 1832, was architecturally in complete contrast to the decrepit seventeenth-century market house shown here. It was a classical forum, designed by Charles Fowler, the architect of the new Covent Garden market buildings, and was soon linked to the South Bank by a suspension bridge for pedestrians engineered by Brunel. However, the merchandise offered did not differ much, to judge from Mayhew's description[33] of the market in the 1850's. To reach Hungerford Stairs, he wrote, one "must pass through the market of the same name . . . known as the great West-end emporium for fish (including periwinkles and shrimps), flesh, and fowl. This classic spot was formerly remarkable for its periwinkle market, the glory of which, however, has now altogether departed." After displays of Epping butter and hot meat and fruit pies come "the poulterers' shops, with the live cocks and hens in coops, and the scarlet combs and black plumage of the birds peeping through the wicker-baskets at the door, while dead geese, with their limp fluffy necks, are hanging over the shelves of the open shop."

In 1859 the new market was in its turn demolished to make way for Charing Cross Station. The bridge was dismantled and its chains taken to Bristol, to be used for the famous Clifton Bridge for which they had originally been intended. The great brick and stone piers, however, remain and still help to support the railway bridge which has preserved the name.

Museum of London; 193 × 261 mm

Digging up Fleet Street

PLATE 31

In 1845 most of London's sewers still discharged their contents directly into the Thames. In spite of increasing public concern, it took another thirteen years, 25,000 deaths from cholera and the 'summer stinks' of the 1850's before the Metropolitan Board of Works, created in 1855, was empowered to construct an efficient system of intercepting main drainage. Until then the building of new sewers, like that shown in Frederick's drawing, brought little improvement in public health. The new Fleet Street sewer, replacing one which had become inadequate, was constructed at a depth of 17 to 25 feet from the surface by Messrs Ward and Son of Aldersgate Street; it cost £2000, but only served to carry the sewage of the area more rapidly into the river.

This watercolour and another, a dramatic view from the bottom of the trench, were based on sketches by Thomas Hosmer dated October 1845. Both were reproduced as wood-engravings to illustrate a brief article in the *Illustrated London News* of 4 October 1845. "The works in progress", it stated, ". . . have attracted considerable attention, partially from the obstruction which they have presented to the public traffic"—hardly an overstatement.

Guildhall Library; 178 × 177 mm

French Horn Yard, High Holborn

It seems hard to credit that as recently as 1850 London still abounded with picturesque taverns and galleried inns like the French Horn; Thomas Hosmer recorded at least 75 of them. His caption dates this inn to the reign of Elizabeth, whereas the features shown are seventeenth-century. By 1851 it had come down in the world, and the yard was devoted to humbler purposes; no carriers operated from it—the bale addressed to Crace is merely a pleasing touch of artist's licence. The public house fronting on to High Holborn now went under the name of the *York Arms*, thus disassociating itself from the squalor behind.

British Museum: Department of Prints and Drawings (Crace Collection); 176 × 228 mm

The slums of the Fleet

PLATES 33 AND 34

Some of London's most ancient slums lay huddled together on the slopes of the Fleet valley. Saffron Hill and Field Lane were already crowded when the steady drift of population from the provinces into London began to quicken in the late eighteenth century. Lord Shaftesbury drew a vivid picture[34] of the first impressions of a country boy:

He alights—and is instantly directed, for the best accommodation, to Duck Lane, St Giles's, Saffron Hill, Spitalfields, or Whitechapel. He reaches the indicated region through tight avenues of glittering fish and rotten vegetables, with doorways or alleys gaping on either side—which, if they be not choked with squalid garments or sickly children, lead the eye through an almost interminable vista of filth and distress . . .

The innocent-sounding West Street, also known by the even less sinister name of Chick Lane, in fact rivalled the rookeries of St Giles' as a breeding-ground of vice and crime. The quiet drabness of its seventeenth-century façade concealed a welter of courts and ramshackle tenements, between which the Fleet flowed as a partly open sewer, bringing damp and disease. Thomas Hosmer's drawing speaks for itself; he made it from a yard behind the Red Lion, West Street, a notorious haunt of thieves and prostitutes. The little group in the foreground are a family of rag-gatherers sorting the results of their morning's collection which lie spread on the ground; according to Mayhew a rag-gatherer's average earnings amounted to between sixpence and eightpence a day, while a night in a common lodging-house, with or without a bed, cost twopence to fourpence.

The small, probably seventeenth-century building shown in Thomas Hosmer's other drawing, unequivocally captioned 'Thieves' lodging house', was one of a number of common lodging houses in Blackboys Alley which wound its way northwards from West Street. Thieves or not, in 1852 nearly 50,000 people lodged nightly in such houses. On 11 February 1834 the *Morning Chronicle* carried a report of the revealing inquest on James Parkinson, aged 36, found dead in a West Street lodging-house:

Mary Wood being sworn, deposed that she was the landlady. . . . The deceased occasionally lodged with her, and he was a dealer in cat's meat. On Tuesday last he came home and asked her for a light, and proceeded to his bedroom. On the Wednesday witness proceeded upstairs to make the beds, when she saw the deceased apparently asleep, but she did not speak to him. On the Thursday . . . she again saw the deceased lying as if asleep, but she did not disturb him . . .

Questioned further she admitted that the room contained eight beds, each occupied by two or three persons, although the deceased had a bed to himself. A juror commented that it was strange that none of his fellow lodgers had realised that Parkinson was dead, to which she simply replied: "No, Sir, they go in and out without seeming to care for each other".

(a) Greater London Council Print Collection; 177 × 227 mm
(b) British Museum: Department of Prints and Drawings (Crace Collection); 166 × 224 mm

a

b

A London prison

PLATE 35

There were no fewer than eleven prisons in mid-Victorian London, most of them built after 1800. Thomas Hosmer's drawing (*c.* 1852) almost certainly shows one of them, although it has so far defied identification. Although the metropolitan prisons were frequently altered and rebuilt in an attempt to improve their efficiency, and the effectiveness of the various penal systems were constantly debated, in 1862 Mayhew and Binny could write:[35] "Our felon population increases . . . as fast as fungi in a rank and foetid atmosphere."

Museum of London; 165 × 228 mm

Alleyn's Almshouses, Bath Street, City Road

PLATE 36

This is another scene familiar to Thomas Hosmer from his childhood a stone's throw away in Ratcliff Row. The Almshouses were founded in 1620 'nye to the Pesthouse' by Edward Alleyn, the prosperous actor who was a contemporary of Shakespeare, better remembered as the founder of Dulwich College. As joint owner of the nearby Fortune Theatre in Golden Lane, he must have known the area well. The inmates were to be of either sex, and were to receive sixpence a week and a coat or gown every other year.

Thomas Hosmer's 1851 drawing shows the almshouses as rebuilt in 1707. They might be in a different world from the Great Exhibition which was taking place only a few miles away. The 1851 census paints an interesting picture of the inmates. The accommodation was adequate and the rules few, to judge from the fact that John Smith at number 2 and Thomas Mayhew at number 10 had relatives living with them and Margaret Gilbert at number 9 even had a resident servant. They were however among the oldest occupants, and may have needed looking after. The men had formerly been employed in watchmaking and engraving, traditional occupations in the Clerkenwell area. The goods displayed on the barrow are shellfish, perhaps pickled whelks.

This drawing is one of many views of almshouses commissioned by Frederick Crace in the early 1850's. It was almost certainly Crace who added the date—1851—to Thomas Hosmer's signature: similar pencilled-in dates occur on many Crace Collection drawings and can be accepted as reliable.

British Museum: Department of Prints and Drawings (Crace Collection); 159 × 293 mm

Aldgate Pump

PLATE 37

Unlike certain other pumps in the heart of London, most notorious among which was the Broad Street pump in Soho which was proved to have been the source of a severe outbreak of cholera, the elegant eighteenth-century Aldgate Pump drew its wholesome supplies from a natural spring known in earlier times as St Michael's Well.

This part of the City escaped the Great Fire, and a number of sixteenth- and seventeenth-century houses survived there until Victorian times. One of these was 74 Leadenhall Street, the timber-framed building to the right of the pump. It had already been emptied of its last occupants, the Terry family who ran a cookshop there, and was demolished shortly after Thomas Hosmer drew it in 1853. The long-established optician's next door at 34 Aldgate Within had since 1835 been in the hands of Henry Macrae, who in spite of his name was a Londoner born in Stepney.

SPECTICALS is a good example of Thomas Hosmer's occasional difficulties with spelling; on another version of this watercolour he rendered it as SPECTICLES.

Greater London Council Print Collection; 190 × 237 mm

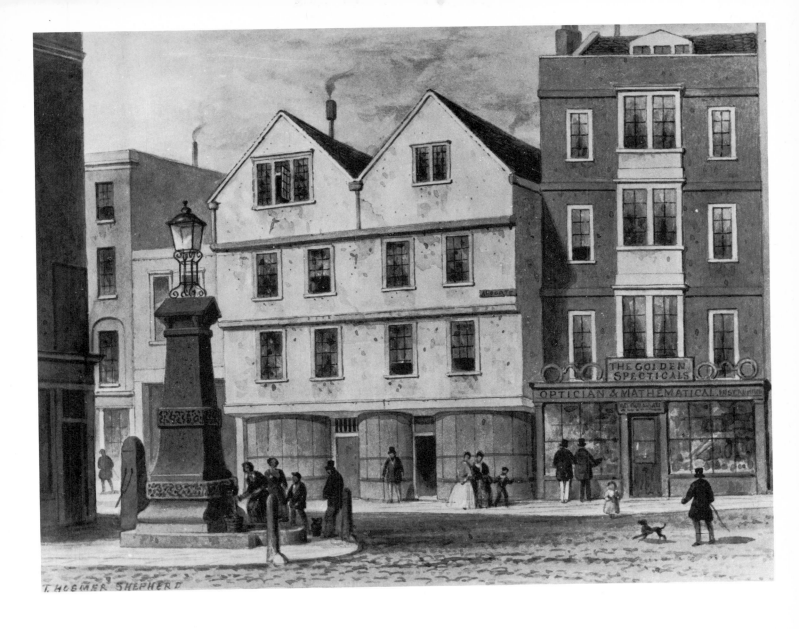

THE GOLDEN
SPECTICALS
OPTICIAN & MATHEMATICAL INSTRUMENT

T. HOSMER SHEPHERD

The Alhambra, Leicester Square

PLATE 38

Thomas Hosmer's watercolour, drawn in 1855 when the Alhambra was fresh and new, shows why it is still remembered, nearly 40 years after its destruction, as one of London's outstanding Victorian buildings. It was opened in 1854, under the best possible auspices, as the *Royal Panopticon of Science and Art*. Its aims, according to the royal charter of 1850 under which it was set up, were

To exhibit and illustrate, in a popular form, discoveries in science and art, to extend the knowledge of useful and ingenious inventions, to promote and illustrate the application of science to the useful arts . . .

The prospectus continued:

Here the artisan and mechanic may learn how to avail themselves of the discoveries and invention of the master-minds who have taken the lead in their own pursuits. The artist may take the initiative from the admirable works around him . . . The manufacturer, by devoting a few hours weekly to the enunciations of the chemical professor . . . will be better prepared to meet . . . competition . . . The agriculturist . . . may at once determine the quality of soils, and the value of the thousand-and-one species of manure offered to his notice . . .

Neither its combination of high ideals with practical aspirations, nor its impressive array of gadgets—the artesian well, the coloured fountain, the diving apparatus, the lift, the electrical machines and the organ—could ensure the success of the Royal Panopticon. In 1858 the contents were cleared out, a stage put in, and under the more appropriate name of the *Alhambra* it became the most splendid music hall in England. Ballets and circuses alternated with variety programmes which on occasion featured the great French gymnast Leotard, who on his second visit in 1866 received a salary of £180 a week. In 1882 the Alhambra was burnt down and rebuilt in the same style; it survived until 1936, to be replaced by the monotonous black glass of the Odeon.

On the extreme left there is a glimpse of an institution which entertained and edified the public with much greater success than the Royal Panopticon. Wylde's *Great Globe*, inside which the earth's surface was shown in relief, occupied the centre of the Square from 1851 to 1861.

British Museum: Department of Prints and Drawings (Crace Collection); 197 × 250 mm

ROYAL PANOPTICON OF SCIENCE & ART.

T.HOSMER.SHEPHERD - 1855

Caron's Almshouses, Wandsworth Road, Vauxhall

PLATE 39

The cottagey appearance of these almshouses harks back to the time when Vauxhall was in the country, still separated from Westminster by a mile of open ground and the width of the unbridged Thames. They were founded by Sir Noel Caron, formerly Dutch ambassador to the courts of Elizabeth and James I, who retired to Vauxhall in 1617 and died there in 1624. In the seventeenth century they must have been a pleasant place in which to end one's days, with the road in front and a field behind running down to the river, but hardly so in 1852: the twin chimneys belonged to the Phoenix Gas Works, and the large building on the left was Price's Belmont candle factory, soon to be extended over the site of the almshouses. A combination of access by water and cheap land had brought rapid industrial development in the Thameside areas of Lambeth and Vauxhall; to the west, railway yards now covered the former market gardens of Battersea.

The last inmates of the almshouses, five widows and two spinsters whose ages ranged from 65 to 78, form an interesting group. Although all must have had long connections with Lambeth to qualify for this parish charity, only four were born in the London area, none of them in Lambeth. The other three came from as far afield as New Romney, Winchcombe in the Cotswolds and St Austell in Cornwall.

Caron's and Alleyn's almshouses (pl. 36) were two of some seventy London almshouses recorded by Thomas Hosmer during the last ten years of his working life up to 1859. In most cases the original drawing, commissioned by Frederick Crace, was followed by one or more variants or copies for other collectors. This watercolour is dated May 1852, but there is a brilliant 1855 copy of the original pencil sketch in the Greater London Council Print Collection which was probably made for Gardner.

British Museum: Department of Prints and Drawings (Crace Collection); 152 × 253 mm

T. HOSMER SHEPHERD

Gun Dock, Wapping

PLATE 40

Wapping came into existence during Stow's lifetime, and one cannot do better than quote the terse description of it in his *Survey of London* (1598):

The usual place for hanging of pirates and sea-rovers, at the low-water mark, and there to remain till three tides had overflowed them; was never a house standing within these forty years, but since the gallows being afterwards removed farther off, a continual street, or filthy street passage, with alleys of small tenements or cottages built, inhabited by sailor's victuallers, along by the river of Thames, almost to Radcliffe, a good mile from the Tower.

Execution Dock lay a short distance downstream of Gun Dock, which was close to Wapping Old Stairs. The area had not changed greatly by 1688, when the notorious Lord Chancellor (Judge) Jeffreys lay hidden in a pot-house, the *Red Cow* in Anchor and Hope Alley, awaiting a chance to escape abroad. He had disguised himself as an ordinary seaman and had shaved off his memorable bushy eyebrows, but one of his erstwhile victims recognized him and Jeffreys was nearly lynched before he could be conveyed to the Tower. A possibly more significant discovery occurred here in the early nineteenth century, when an unusual plant on a Wapping window-sill caught the eye of an observant nurseryman. It was a fuchsia, then unknown in this country, which a sailor had brought home from the West Indies.

Thomas Hosmer produced this watercolour in 1850; the original pencil sketch, now in the Guildhall Library, is more vivid but drawn in so soft a pencil that, as with the majority of Thomas Hosmer's sketches, reproduction cannot do it justice. Lloyd's Register contains no record of a three-masted *Bell*, so the name may be that of the proprietor rather than of the vessel.

British Museum: Department of Prints and Drawings (Crace Collection); 164 × 250 mm

The Halfway House

PLATE 41

This rural-looking inn was a sight familiar to travellers on the road to Bath, a sure sign that they were leaving London behind. Its name refers to the fact that it lay halfway between the City and Hammersmith. It stood on the north side of Kensington Road, backing onto the wall of Hyde Park, opposite what is now the north end of Ennismore Gardens.

By the time that Thomas Hosmer drew the Halfway House, some time in the early 1840's, the opposite side of the road was lined with houses, but when it was first built in the early eighteenth century it stood almost alone. This part of the road was a noted haunt of footpads, some of whom may well have used the inn, since during its demolition a secret staircase was discovered leading from an upper room to the stables. Thomas Hosmer's affectionate portrayal of the old house, which he must often have passed on his way to visit Crace at Hammersmith, would not have appealed to the fashionable inhabitants of Kensington Gore who regarded it as an eyesore and an obstruction in the roadway. It was eventually removed in 1846 at a cost of £3050. This watercolour, presumably based on earlier sketches, dates from about 1854, to judge from style and signature (not shown). It has the best qualities of his late work: although the drawing is less vigorous the eye for detail remains, together with a certain undemonstrative charm.

Kensington Central Library: Local History Collection; 165 × 240 mm

Cheyne Walk, looking west: evening

PLATE 42

No-one has ever captured the atmosphere of Cheyne Walk with more verve and exactness than Thomas Carlyle. Writing to his wife in 1834, just before they came to live at 5 Cheyne Row, he described it as

running along the shore of the river, a broad highway with huge shady trees, boats lying moored, and a smell of shipping and tar. Battersea Bridge (of wood) a few yards off; the broad river, with white-trousered, white-shirted Cockneys, dashing by like arrows in their long canoes of boats; beyond, the green beautiful knolls of Surrey with their villages. On the whole a most artificial green-painted yet lively fresh almost opera-looking business as you can fancy.

The Carlyles were still living in Cheyne Row, running back from the river behind the end of the trees, when Thomas Hosmer painted this watercolour, about 1857. He made his sketches from the Cadogan Pier, a boarding point for steamers which projected a short distance into the Thames where Albert Bridge now crosses it. The wherries drawn up on the foreshore remind one that Cheyne Walk still enjoyed a close relationship with and dependence on the river. Beyond Battersea Bridge were boatyards, one of them owned by the Greaves family who had often ferried Turner and whose youngest member Walter was himself to become a memorable artist. Between the Old Church and the river barges lie on the mud alongside Arch House Wharf where the energetic Mrs Isabella Alldin ran her coal yard. Only the variety of little businesses along the Walk—among them coffee rooms, a toy warehouse, a printer and a pawnbroker—suggest the growing population in the streets behind. All this was utterly transformed by the construction in 1874 of the Chelsea Embankment, which divorced Cheyne Walk from the river and took away all the intimacy of the scene.

Chelsea Library: Local History Collection; 167 × 253 mm

F. OSMER Shepherd

152

83

Ewer Street, Gravel Lane, Southwark

PLATE 43

'A very remarkable place', wrote Thomas Hosmer on one of his 1852 drawings of Ewer Street. Even allowing for a touch of irony, this was a fair description. Its wooden houses, modest enough in their original late seventeenth-century setting among fields and tenter grounds, had deteriorated into a verminous slum flanked by railways, iron foundries and a starch factory. The houses shown here are numbers 1 (at the far end) to 13; the 1851 census lists a total of 181 occupants, ranging from a couple at number 1 to 43 at number 9, the larger building in the centre, which was a lodging house. Its inmates consisted of 8 families and 16 single individuals, including boys of 12 and 14. Over a third of the inhabitants of numbers 1–13 were Irish, some, no doubt, refugees from the famine of the 1840's. The people of Ewer Street pursued over 60 different occupations, some of them related, a reminder that London, unlike most other great British cities, was not dominated by a few major industries. Besides labourers, market traders, porters and charwomen, there were foundrymen, shoemakers, printers and bookbinders and a dealer in hearthstones; hatmaking and leatherworking, both traditional local activities, were also represented.

A contemporary newspaper article[36] confirms the implications of the census figures: "Ewer Street, during the intense hot weather of the last summer, presented at night a sickening and humiliating spectacle. The houses . . . are literally *alive with vermin*, and the wretched occupiers were actually driven out of doors . . . and at nightfall, for weeks and months, were to be seen sleeping huddled together on the doorsteps, and on the footways . . ."

Greater London Council Print Collection; 168 × 247 mm

Smithfield Bars

PLATE 44

This was the cattle drover's first glimpse of Smithfield, as after winding his way from Islington down the interminable length of St John Street he entered the broad open space of the market. Its smell and noise and the vile effluvia of its many slaughter houses pervaded a wide area until it was removed to the new Caledonian Market at Islington in 1855. Although the market itself had gone, Thomas Hosmer's 1857 drawing still contains many reminders of it: Spill and Company's waterproof clothing business rubs shoulders with Edgington's who make rickcloths and tarpaulins as well as marquees, and beyond them is the veterinary chemist John Cayley. These buildings, ancient timber-framed structures beneath their Georgianized facades, were cleared away for the new dead-meat market, opened in 1868. In the background can be seen the classical pediment of Bart's and the pinnacled tower of St Sepulchre, Skinner Street; St Paul's is just out of sight on the left.

Executed with some care and signed, this drawing is clearly intended as a work in its own right rather than just a sketch, although there is a watercolour of the same subject. It is one of a series on the ancient boundaries of the City which Thomas Hosmer produced between 1857 and 1859. Smithfield Bars took its name from the wooden barrier which during the Middle Ages was used to control access to the City at this point.

Guildhall Library; 163 × 246 mm

Garden Row, Islington

PLATE 45

One of the original back lanes of the old village of Islington, Garden or Hedge Row skirted the gardens of houses on the west side of Upper Street. Until the construction of the Agricultural Hall in 1861–2 swallowed up the whole site, there was a sizeable patch of open ground, shown in Frederick's watercolour, lying between Garden Row and Liverpool Road and directly opposite the east end of Chapman Street where the Shepherds lived. In the distance can be seen the steeple of the parish church of St Mary where Frederick and most of his younger brothers and sisters were baptized.

Frederick and his father drew this field and the sheds and fences adjoining it several times. One suspects that it was a favourite playground of the Shepherd children which they recorded for sentimental reasons not long before its final disappearance.

Greater London Council Print Collection; 162 × 215 mm

City Boundry Smithfield Bars 1857

The Gun Tavern, Buckingham Gate

PLATE 46

Before it was built over and became the poor relation of Mayfair and Belgravia, Pimlico was known for its market gardens and suburban inns. The Gun Tavern, on the south side of Buckingham Gate not far from Buckingham Palace, was one of the oldest of these. This watercolour, drawn in 1857, the year of its demolition, shows the rear of the inn; it is typical of the many drawings of threatened buildings made by Thomas Hosmer during his last, most prolific period.

Archives Department, Westminster City Libraries; 175 × 232 mm

The Racket Ground, Fleet Prison

PLATE 47

The triangular yard behind the main block of the Fleet was known as the 'Bare', or racket ground. There the prisoners compensated for their enforced idleness by playing a variety of games, including rackets, shown here, fives, tennis and skittles. These facilities were supervised by a Racket Master and a Skittle Master, elected annually by the prisoners from among themselves. The offices were eagerly sought after, since the holders were entitled to claim fees in return for supplying bats and balls, and candidates even issued handbills setting out their qualifications for the posts.

This drawing illustrates the complex and sometimes devious origins of some of Frederick's later drawings. In making it he may have drawn on personal impressions of the Fleet gathered before its closure in 1842; he clearly also had in mind Pugin and Rowlandson's view of the same subject in *The Microcosm of London* (1808). That he was not copying directly from their work is shown by his treatment of the rail fence on the left. In the *Microcosm* this is the low wooden surround of a skittle alley, whereas in Frederick's drawing it has become a meaningless enclosure. Frederick's figures owe nothing to Rowlandson; they are broken-down swells of the kind he often portrayed. Their dress and the style of the drawing suggest that it dates from after 1850. The carefully-observed artist with his Garibaldi hat could well be a self-portrait—if so, it is our only clue to what the Shepherds looked like, apart from the wood-engraving showing Thomas Hosmer at work. This possibility is strengthened by the fact that Frederick's signature, a light red FS in monogram which does not reproduce in black and white, is placed on the fence post close to the figure.

Greater London Council Print Collection; 173 × 191 mm

Old houses, King Street, Westminster

PLATE 48

King Street ran slightly west of and parallel to the line of the present Parliament Street. Forming part of the umbilical cord of Fleet Street, the Strand and Whitehall linking the City to the royal enclave of Westminster, houses were already lining its western side at the beginning of Queen Elizabeth's reign. When T. H. Shepherd produced this watercolour in May 1858 the street's days appeared to be numbered. In fact, although the north half was cleared away soon afterwards to make way for the Home Office, the houses shown here, numbers 34, 33 and 32 on the west side, survived until the very end of the nineteenth century when their site was covered by the government offices fronting onto Parliament Square.

Suppliers of a variety of goods and services had clustered here around the fringes of government. Blue Boar's Head Yard, entered beneath the pub, contained a builders' yard, livery stables, three cab proprietors and a coach painter. Numbers 33 and 32, early eighteenth-century at the front but probably older behind, housed Mrs Ann Johnston's bakery, John Vodden's barber's shop and Edwin Lavers's coffee and chop house. In earlier days King Street was noted for its coffee houses; Pepys regularly records the latest scrap of court gossip which he has picked up there, and in *The Compleat Angler* (1676) Piscator says: 'When I dress an eel thus, I will he was as long and big as that which was caught in Peterboro' river in the year 1667, which was $3\frac{3}{4}$ feet long; if you will not believe me, then go and see it at one of the coffee-houses in King Street'.

Lord Howard of Effingham, Edmund Spenser and Wenceslas Hollar were among the famous people who lived here, close to the source of power and influence. On the site of Lavers's coffee house, or even perhaps in the actual building, Oliver Cromwell installed his aged mother until her death in 1654. A year or two later, while his coach was held up by a crush of people in the narrow street, a would-be assassin was detected, lurking with drawn sword behind the half-closed shutters of a shop. In 1665, the shadow of the Plague fell early on King Street: on 28 June Pepys wrote, "In my way to Westminster Hall, I observed several plague-houses (i.e. houses sealed up because of outbreaks) in King Street and the Palace".

British Museum: Department of Prints and Drawings (Crace Collection); 224 × 206 mm

The Pottery at Belle Isle

PLATE 49

York Road, King's Cross is a bleak sight today, making its way northwards between the vast railway cutting and the disused warehouses along the Regent's Canal. It was very different in 1832. Known then as Maiden Lane, it soon left the houses behind and climbed towards Highgate between fields and market gardens. On the rising ground nearby, called Belle Isle, commanding wide views in all directions, stood two small potteries; the rich deposits of brick-earth in this part of London were thoroughly exploited before being themselves covered by bricks and mortar.

This large elaborate watercolour is very probably the painting entitled *The Pottery at Belle Isle* which George Sidney showed at the Society of British Artists in 1833. It demonstrates his aspirations and the reasons for his ultimate failure. To achieve this carefully composed, academic picture, George Sidney had to rearrange the local topography. The note 'painted on the spot' probably refers only to the main subject; the background was doubtless completed in the studio.

The atmosphere is immediately established by the towering kilns, which explain the foreground where clay is being worked to the right consistency for moulding. George Sidney has raised it above the level of its immediate surroundings, adding on the left a jumble of buildings which did not exist in 1832. However, the distinctively pinnacled church on the skyline is undoubtedly Holy Trinity, Cloudesley Square, Islington, built in 1826. The fine setting shows up the inadequacy of George Sidney's figure drawing, so that the resulting picture is weak by comparison with for instance, Linnell's *Kensington Gravel Pits* (1813).

Victoria and Albert Museum: Department of Prints and Drawings; 318 × 416 mm

The Haunted House, Gravel Lane

PLATE 50

From 1860 onwards the second railway boom wrought havoc in north-western Southwark. By 1866, when Frederick drew its demolition, this fine late seventeenth-century house was flanked grotesquely by the South-Eastern and Chatham Railway from Charing Cross which was itself crossed at a higher level (extreme left) by the London, Chatham and Dover Railway coming out of Blackfriars. Like many another large, neglected mansion it had acquired a sinister reputation, for which there was no apparent foundation. Frederick's drawing is related to a fine wood-engraving published in the summer of 1866.

Greater London Council Print Collection; 202 × 227 mm

Burford's Panorama, Cranbourn Street

PLATE 51

The combination of entertainment with instruction, epitomised by the Great Exhibition and often regarded as an essentially Victorian concept, first appeared much earlier. It formed the basis of several flourishing institutions in late Georgian London, of which the sole survivor is Madame Tussaud's. One of the earliest and most interesting was the *Eidophusikon*, developed by the painter Philip de Loutherbourg who pioneered many innovations in stage design at Drury Lane. In one of its displays changing effects of light projected onto a panorama suggested the passage of the day, from dawn to dusk.

In 1793 what was to be the most famous of all panoramas opened in Cranbourn Street, just off Leicester Square. Thomas Barker, an Irish-born portrait painter working in Edinburgh, had conceived the idea of displaying a panoramic view around the walls of a circular gallery to achieve a more realistic effect. He patented his invention, and in 1789 brought to London a panorama of Edinburgh which crowds flocked to see. His panorama of London from Albion Mills, Blackfriars Bridge, first exhibited in 1792, was so successful that it was even published as a series of aquatints. The following year he leased a site off Cranbourn Street and erected three circular galleries, the largest of which, ninety feet in diameter and forty feet high, can be seen in Thomas Hosmer's watercolour.

The new building opened with a view of the Fleet at Spithead, and sustained public interest in the great set-piece battles of the Napoleonic Wars set the seal on Barker's success. He died in 1806, but his son Henry carried on the business; from his panorama of Waterloo alone he is said to have made £10,000. Many of the views were painted by the Barkers' pupil John Burford and his son Robert, and in 1823 Henry Barker transferred to them the management of his two establishments (the other was in the Strand), living on comfortably until 1856.

The Burfords were incredibly energetic. Between 1823 and 1858 they exhibited some 86 panoramas, famous cities and picturesque scenes alternating with subjects of more topical interest. These were prepared in a special circular studio close to Robert Burford's home in Kentish Town. The Crimean War and the Indian Mutiny gave opportunities unparalleled since the fall of Napoleon, and as Thomas Hosmer's watercolour shows, in 1856–58 *The Fall of Delhi* and *The City of Lucknow* were simultaneous attractions. After being enthralled by them one could restore oneself in James Wylde's adjoining premises, which offered refreshment as well as cigars and newspapers. Numbers 10–15 Leicester Square, a corner of which is visible on the left, was the splendid establishment of Messrs Hampton and Russell, upholsterers. Burford's Panorama finally closed not long before Robert Burford's death in 1861, not without a protest from John Ruskin, who had happy memories of visits to Cranbourn Street as a child and considered that the educational value of the Panorama was so great that it should have been maintained by a government grant. It was converted into a Roman Catholic church, the present Notre Dame de France (rebuilt following war damage).

British Museum: Department of Prints and Drawings (Crace Collection); 224 × 171 mm

LEICESTER SQUARE

14 & 15

R. BURFORD'S

PANORAMA
THE FALL OF DELHI
CITY OF LUCKNOW.

CRANBOURE STREET

WESTERN COA

COFFEE
TEA
TOBACCO
&
CEGARS

T. H. Shepherd 1858

The Clearance for Garrick Street

PLATE 52

Even in the early nineteenth century the inaccessibility of Covent Garden Market was becoming a problem. Access was particularly difficult from the north-west, where heavily-laden carts had to find their way through the narrow streets of Soho. The fact that London still lacked any overall local authority made problems of this kind almost impossible to remedy. The formation of a new street running south-east from the junction of Long Acre and St Martin's Lane was first suggested in 1846; although the need was obvious and the Duke of Bedford, the principal landlord, offered a contribution of £10,000 towards the cost, discussions dragged on and the government, with more pressing matters to consider, never came to a decision.

The project was revived in 1856, shortly after the setting-up of the Metropolitan Board of Works. The creation of Garrick Street was their first venture in street improvement, to be followed by many more including Shaftesbury Avenue and Charing Cross Road. Before laying out the new street the Board held a competition for the best design for its roadway and subterranean services, resulting in the construction of an arched conduit to carry gas and water mains. Thomas Hosmer's watercolour of 1857/8 shows clearance under way at the St Martin's Lane end; by coincidence his youngest son, the wood engraver Valentine Claude, later lived at 2 Garrick Street. He and his young wife Ellen came there about 1870 with their eldest daughter; they remained, ensconced between Petters Hotel and James Murton's boarding house, until about 1884, during which time two more children were born. They then moved a short distance to 20 Cranbourn Street, where Valentine Claude died on 17 January 1888.

Archives Department, Westminster City Libraries; 175 × 249 mm

Overleaf This slightly enlarged section of Shury's *Plan of London* (1832) shows London as it was at the height of T. H. Shepherd's career, and includes most of the family's homes and the places shown in their drawings (Greater London Council Map Collection).

99

The Shepherds' London Drawings: a Guide

The Shepherds still offer considerable opportunities to collectors. At present there is confusion about Thomas Hosmer: unsigned watercolours freely—and almost invariably wrongly—attributed to him fetch inflated prices, while his pencil sketches are often unrecognised and can be bought very cheaply. This *Guide*, used in conjunction with the plates, should help in the identification and dating of genuine drawings.

The Shepherds had no direct predecessors. Influences are discernible: in his treatment of architecture and in the way in which he infused it with human interest George was a distant follower of distinguished older contemporaries like Rooker and Hearne. The street scenes of Thomas Malton II, published in his *Picturesque Tour through London and Westminster* (1792), clearly influenced Thomas Hosmer, although his major set-pieces combine accurate drawing with a vivid atmosphere quite unlike Malton. The growing demand for illustrated topography required this combination of accuracy and a sense of place, and the Shepherds' work was a response to this demand. Hardie[37] classes them as architectural draftsmen in company with better known academic figures like Augustus Charles Pugin and Frederick Mackenzie; they can also be compared with other contemporaries like William Pearson and John Coney[38] whose architectural drawings were similar but more pedestrian. As artists, the Shepherds were of limited importance; it is the content of their work which makes them significant.

George Shepherd

The earliest drawing by George Shepherd which I have been able to trace is dated 1801.[6] A pencil sketch of old buildings in the Barbican, it already displays a well-developed ability to suggest space and texture, and is carefully captioned and dated in his attractive round hand. George's pencil work is hardly ever signed, and apart from its relationship to watercolours the almost invariable presence of his handwriting provides the only sure means of identification. By contrast, almost all his finished watercolours bear the simple signature *G. Shepherd*, often followed by the date, and unsigned watercolours attributed to him should be treated with caution. He is frequently confused with George Shephe*a*rd, a contemporary who drew similar subjects, usually in gouache rather than pure watercolour. Stylistic differences aside, the latter's tendency to sign his work with the initials G.S., sometimes in monogram, is a reliable means of distinguishing it from that of George.

The major collections contain only nine drawings by him prior to 1809; one of these is a watercolour of Stepney Church, dated 1803,[39] which is still eighteenth-century in manner. By the time that he began actively to draw London his own distinctive style was fully formed. His assured pen and pencil drawings are very effective; occasionally an excessive meticulousness creeps in, but generally he succeeds admirably in conveying the subtly varied texture of London architecture, notably the diversity of brick. His watercolours reveal two divergent tendencies. George could express most eloquently the quiet tones of London;

there is a moving pathos in his large drawing of Drury Lane Theatre (pl. 3), its ruins exposed to the pale February light. At the same time his work reveals a robust interest in the vivid, almost coarse local colour which abounded in pre-Victorian London, demonstrated in his 1815 watercolour of Clare Market (pl. 11). Most of George's London drawings of the 1810's were commissioned for eventual publication in *Londina Illustrata*, *Architectura Ecclesiastica Londini* and other works. One interesting series never apparently engraved is a group of drawings of City livery halls, perhaps prepared for a collector of London topography. George's drawings were also in demand as extra illustrations for standard works; most extra-illustrated sets of Pennant's *London* contain some, particularly the magnificent set prepared for Henry Fauntleroy now in Sir John Soane's Museum.

From 1816 onwards George appears to have done fewer drawings of London, and I have been unable to trace any dated between 1821 and 1825. He seems to have virtually given up the preparation of drawings for engraving, concentrating instead on topographical work in various parts of southern England. Even during his period of greatest activity in London, George had continued to sketch in Bedfordshire and Hertfordshire, and a series of drawings[11] made during his tour in 1819 in Berkshire and Oxfordshire reveal an aspect of his *oeuvre* not apparent in his London work. These are panoramic views of small country towns like Banbury and Chipping Norton, executed with great verve in a sepia wash. Although the summer countryside is beautifully evoked in these drawings, the central, dominant interest is provided by the townscape, where the Shepherds' real calling lay. George spent much time in his later years drawing subjects far removed from urban topography, but without real success; whether coastal scenes, studies of cattle on Primrose Hill or his numerous views of south Devon, they never contain the conviction which only the texture of buildings could draw from him. However, exhibition catalogues from 1830 onwards show that both George and his younger son George Sidney painted genre scenes and still lifes— *Ballad singers*, *Shelling peas*, *Study of weeds* and *Dead game* are typical titles—and these may have been effective, to judge from a comic drawing by Thomas Hosmer entitled *The Baker's Round*, showing a baker drinking at an inn.[40] However, when George attempted to place a genre subject in the foreground of a topographical drawing, as in his exquisite 1825 view of the Vale of Health (pl. 16), the two elements do not marry convincingly.

At the very end of his career, in 1828, George began a further series of London drawings. Although these tiny wash or watercolour views, measuring approximately 60 × 95 mm., look as though they were prepared for engraving, I have been unable to trace any publication in which they appeared. Their exciting quality (see pl. 26) proves that as he neared sixty George's eyesight was undimmed and townscape could still draw a deep response from him.

Thomas Hosmer Shepherd

Unlike his father, whose style changed measurably over the 30-odd years of his career, Thomas Hosmer's style altered remarkably little, and drawings made by him in 1814 and 1859 are recognisably the work of the same artist. By his early 20s he had developed an effective topographical technique which served him well and which he had no need to modify. Apart from scattered plates in

Londina Illustrata, Thomas Hosmer's earliest drawings were produced for Ackermann's magazine *The Repository of the Arts*. Between 1809 and 1815 he and his father contributed some 35 drawings of London scenes which were reproduced as coloured aquatints. These were used again in 1816 as illustrations to J. B. Papworth's *Select Views of London*. In both instances these plates appeared without any indication of artist or engraver, unlike the remaining illustrations to Papworth's book and most other Ackermann productions. Extant drawings and outline etchings enable 19 of the 35 aquatints in question to be positively attributed, 2 to George and 17 to Thomas Hosmer. All 35 plates were etched by the same skilful hand, with such faithfulness to the surviving drawings that a further 16 plates can be attributed to the partnership of father and son on grounds of style alone.

The engraver was none other than Thomas Hosmer himself. On the outline etching[25] which he prepared for the 1814 aquatint of St Clement Danes is his signature, neatly etched across the bottom left-hand corner. It can still be detected on examples of the finished plate, only partly obscured by aquatint ground. On another outline etching,[16] for the 1814 view of the Old Bailey, his flowing *TH Shepherd del* is etched in the empty area of the plate beneath the design. In engraving his own and, apparently, his father's work, Thomas Hosmer was following in the footsteps of many distinguished artists who were equally at home with the pencil and the graver. He seems virtually to have ceased engraving after 1815, once his efficiency as a supplier of topographical drawings had been recognised, but was responsible for two pairs of small plates in *London in the Nineteenth Century* (see below). His grasp of the techniques involved is reflected in the extraordinary precision with which his drawings were translated into plates. In their turn all three of his sons took to engraving.

Almost all of Thomas Hosmer's vast output of drawings are small, usually no larger than 150 × 250 mm. The nine large drawings of London scenes which were engraved and published as Ackermann aquatints between 1816 and 1822 show that he could create successful designs on a larger scale (approximately 330 × 490 mm) than we usually associate with him. They also reveal a greater deftness in the characterisation and placing of figures than George ever achieved. However, it is through the 352 engravings for *Metropolitan Improvements* and *London in the Nineteenth Century* that Thomas Hosmer is best known, and the drawings and signed proofs for these shed light on his methods of working. He began by making one or more pencil sketches on the spot (pl. 19), which are usually captioned in his hand and precisely dated; from these he prepared a sepia wash drawing (pl. 18), almost always signed and often dated, which was then etched and engraved on steel. The two volumes were issued in parts, and between four and nine months elapsed between the preparation of a drawing and its publication as an engraving, except towards the end of each volume when the interval was sometimes as brief as two months, suggesting that artist and engravers were under pressure to complete the task. Annotations by Thomas Hosmer on his signed proofs[16] of *London in the Nineteenth Century* imply that he worked closely with the engravers, of whom over forty were employed on the two volumes. Some of them he had probably known for years, since they had worked on Wilkinson's *Londina Illustrata* for which he and his father had made drawings. It is possible that he was at least partly responsible for making arrangements for the engraving, since on one proof he comments, 'Mottram [the engraver] cheap £10.0.0', and on another, 'W.B.[arber, the engraver] says this cloud has caused as much labour as all the rest of the subject'. As *London in the Nineteenth Century* neared completion, Thomas Hosmer helped out by himself engraving two pairs of small subjects, plates 165 and 188.

The mass of London drawings which he had accumulated by the age of 38 provided Thomas Hosmer with a ready source of material for the remaining 28 years of his career up to 1859. The 395 illustrations, very small and five to a page, which he contributed to *Partington* (1835) are most of them quite obviously derived from his earlier work, from the *Repository of the Arts* onwards, as are a good many of the remaining 152 illustrations by H. West. The sepia wash drawings which Thomas Hosmer made for this work, usually measuring 58 × 48 mm, are unsigned on account of their small size; they are not as well finished as their earlier counterparts. His pencil drawings for *London Interiors* (1841–44) are vigorous and break new ground in that attention is focused on the human activity portrayed as well as on its architectural setting. I have been unable to trace any wash drawings prepared for this series.

More than three-quarters of Thomas Hosmer's 1500 extant London drawings were produced during the last fifteen years of his active life, from 1844 onwards: during 1852 alone he made more than 120. These later drawings are rather different in character from his earlier work. The difference is not one of style—Thomas Hosmer's style altered remarkably little over the years—but of function: his late work was intended not for engraving but to meet the demand from collectors, above all Frederick Crace. Unlike his often untidy preliminary sketches of the later 1820's, the sole function of which was to provide a basis for a wash drawing, Thomas Hosmer's late pencil drawings are executed with some care and often signed. In the watercolours derived from them vivid colour rather than line is used to express the texture of buildings, and there is less concern with the effects of light and shade vital to the engraver. Many of these watercolours exist in three or four almost identical versions, and there is inevitably a certain slickness about them. This does not necessarily mean that they are unreliable as to detail; advancing years did not significantly impair Thomas Hosmer's accuracy as a portrayer of the London scene. Nevertheless, his late sketches and watercolours have to be treated with caution; the demand for them appears to have been so great that he could only meet it by copying earlier material in addition to his current work.

There are various means of identifying these late copies. Many are based on engravings in the two major books; they are invariably larger, whereas Thomas Hosmer's original sketches and wash drawings are the same size as the engravings. Whether originals or copies, most of his late pencil drawings are signed, but originals, although more polished than his earlier sketches, contain corrections and other tell-tale signs whereas copies betray themselves by an overall smoothness and absence of specific detail, particularly in the treatment of walls and road surfaces, although they quite often bear notes of colour and materials like originals. The same bland absence of detail also characterises late watercolours derived from earlier material. Most of Thomas Hosmer's original drawings bear a specific date, for instance *Sep. 27 1837*; on late copies he usually inscribed only the year of the original, adding where applicable the comment 'Now taken down'. In a very few cases he altered the date on a pencil drawing, for example turning 1841 into 1821, but not carefully enough to escape detection.

Thomas Hosmer's signatures: Unlike his father's signature, which changed very little during the course of his career, Thomas Hosmer's signatures vary quite considerably and when used in conjunction with other evidence are useful for dating. The sequence runs as follows.

period	form of signature
1809–1821	*T. H. Shepherd* (*T. Hosmer Shepherd* on some larger drawings)
1821–1847	*T. H. Shepherd* or *Tho. H. Shepherd* (the latter mostly on wash drawings for engraving, and rarely after 1831)
1847–1849	*T. H. Shepherd* or *H Shepherd*
1849–1859	*T. H. Shepherd*, *H Shepherd*, *T. Hosmer Shepherd*, *T. HOSMER Shepherd* or *T. HOSMER SHEPHERD*

The last is the only signature that Thomas Hosmer formed entirely in block letters; forgeries of his signature, of which a number exist, usually follow this form since it is the easiest to copy. The forged signature *T. H. SHEPHERD*, which he never used, also exists. Although Thomas Hosmer failed to sign a few of his watercolours and many of his pencil sketches, I have never come across a genuine drawing to which a forged signature has been added.

George Sidney Shepherd

I have succeeded in tracing twenty of George Sidney's London watercolours ranging in date from 1824 to 1842, and one pencil sketch attributable to him; from so small a sample of his output only the most tentative conclusions can be drawn. This is a pity, since the contrast between George Sidney and the other Shepherds puts both his and their work in perspective.

George Sidney's poignant view of the last of Bagnigge Wells (pl. 23) shows that in mid-career he was still capable of pure topographical drawing in the best Shepherd tradition. Some of his drawings, for instance *Drury Court* (pl. 24), have echoes of his father (compare pl. 1). However, as can be seen from his impression of Smithfield (pl. 14), George Sidney was attempting as early as 1824 to strike out into the mainstream of English watercolour painting. The fluctuation and ultimate decline of his relationship with the New Society of Painters in Watercolours reflects his failure to achieve this aim, but most of the work I have seen succeeds up to a point. Although he was the most technically accomplished of the Shepherds, George Sidney's ideas outran his ability to express them. By the time that he came to make the drawings for the series of lithographs published by Rudolph Ackermann junior in 1851, he was a spent force. They are carefully executed—one fetched £550 at auction in 1970—but uninspired: pl. 7, *The Club Houses, Pall Mall* is a direct plagiarism of T. S. Boys's *London as it is*.

More than half the watercolours I have traced are signed and dated; some bear statements like *Finished on the Spot*. The form of signature is in most cases *Geo. Sidney Shepherd*, but *George Sidney Shepherd*, *Geo. S. Shepherd* and *G.S.S.* also occur.

Frederick Napoleon Shepherd

Frederick Shepherd's pencil and watercolour drawings are relatively uncommon; I have succeeded in tracing less than 200. There is no evidence that he ever worked outside London. His early work prior to 1840, for example the lively view of Old Hungerford Market (pl. 30), is well-executed and exhilarating. The same qualities appear in a series of small watercolours of Islington scenes commissioned by George Daniel of Canonbury, who was compiling an extra-illustrated copy[41] of Nelson's *History . . . of the parish of St Mary Islington* in the late 1830's.

The mysterious and catastrophic change which cut short Frederick's development and turned his work into a pale reflection of his father's took place not long after 1840. From this point onwards the working relationship between father and son was very close. They constantly drew the same subjects, and Thomas Hosmer sometimes captioned Frederick's drawings; some of Frederick's watercolours of the 1840's, for instance pl. 31, are based on drawings by Thomas Hosmer which the latter never seems to have worked up into watercolours himself. Frederick later copied his father's work a good deal, and had access to drawings by his grandfather as well, as is shown by his watercolour copy of a fine drawing of an old house at Putney made by George in 1826.[42] Up to the 1850's Frederick's subjects range widely over central London, with particular emphasis on Islington, but the 38 drawings produced in his final burst of activity between 1871 and 1874 are almost all of streets and buildings between Northumberland House and Covent Garden. They were probably commissioned by the collector J. E. Gardner, whose business premises were in that area, at 454 Strand.

Frederick did not always sign his watercolours and rarely, if ever, his drawings. His signature up to the 1840's is a firm *F.N. Shepherd*; later he dropped the *N*, using *F. Shepherd*, *Fred. Shepherd* or even a monogram of the letters FS.

The Major Collections

Note : Collections are listed in order of importance of their holdings of Shepherd drawings. Conditions of access vary widely, and it is wise to write or telephone in advance of any visit.

BRITISH MUSEUM, DEPARTMENT OF PRINTS AND DRAWINGS: CRACE COLLECTION Includes the largest single group of London drawings by George and Thomas Hosmer, in particular the latter's large drawings for the 1816–1822 aquatints and the best of his late work. Very few by Frederick and none, surprisingly, by George Sidney. Not in the Crace Collection, but extremely interesting, is a large batch of some 80 wash drawings prepared by Thomas Hosmer for *Modern Athens*.

GUILDHALL LIBRARY Several hundred drawings by George, Thomas Hosmer and Frederick; a few by George Sidney. Also an important proof set of the engravings for *London in the Nineteenth Century* signed and annotated by Thomas Hosmer, and copies of *Metropolitan Improvements* and *London in the Nineteenth Century* in parts as originally issued.

GREATER LONDON COUNCIL PRINT COLLECTION, COUNTY HALL Several hundred drawings by all four artists, including much late work by Thomas Hosmer and Frederick. Extra-illustrated copy of Nelson's *History . . . of the parish of St Mary Islington* containing watercolours by Frederick (in Library).

MUSEUM OF LONDON A smaller group of drawings, but of exceptionally fine quality. A few by George; some important work by Thomas Hosmer, including many of the wash drawings for *Metropolitan Improvements* and *London in the Nineteenth Century*. Several drawings by George Sidney and very significant early material by Frederick.

ARCHIVES DEPARTMENT, WESTMINSTER CITY LIBRARIES: (1) WESTMINSTER LOCAL HISTORY COLLECTION, VICTORIA LIBRARY, BUCKINGHAM PALACE ROAD Many drawings by Thomas Hosmer and Frederick, including some attractive late work by the former; some by George, none by George Sidney.
(2) ASHBRIDGE COLLECTION, MARYLEBONE DISTRICT LIBRARY, MARYLEBONE ROAD A few significant drawings by George and Thomas Hosmer.

CHELSEA LOCAL HISTORY COLLECTION, CHELSEA LIBRARY, MANRESA ROAD A fine group, largely late drawings by Thomas Hosmer with a few by Frederick and one unusual gouache by George Sidney.

KENSINGTON LOCAL HISTORY COLLECTION, KENSINGTON CENTRAL LIBRARY, PHILLIMORE WALK Another large group, mainly by Thomas Hosmer and including some good late drawings.

ISLINGTON LOCAL HISTORY COLLECTION: (1) ISLINGTON CENTRAL LIBRARY, HOLLOWAY ROAD Work by Thomas Hosmer and Frederick only, important in view of their local connections. Another extra-illustrated Nelson (see above).

(2) FINSBURY LIBRARY, ST JOHN'S STREET A few drawings by George, Thomas Hosmer and Frederick; the latter's last drawing.

VICTORIA AND ALBERT MUSEUM, DEPARTMENT OF PRINTS AND DRAWINGS A small number of drawings by George, Thomas Hosmer and George Sidney, including the best of the latter's work. Some drawings attributed to Thomas Hosmer are at Bethnal Green Museum (not seen).

HACKNEY LOCAL HISTORY COLLECTION, STOKE NEWINGTON LIBRARY, STOKE NEWINGTON CHURCH STREET Some drawings by Thomas Hosmer (not seen).

SIR JOHN SOANE'S MUSEUM, LINCOLN'S INN FIELDS An extra-illustrated copy of Pennant's . . . *London*, prepared for Henry Fauntleroy, containing a considerable number of drawings by George.

CAMDEN LOCAL HISTORY COLLECTION, CENTRAL REFERENCE LIBRARY, SWISS COTTAGE A few drawings by Thomas Hosmer and one by George Sidney.

The above is by no means a comprehensive list of locations of Shepherd drawings of London. With the exception of those in the Crace Collection and Soane Museum, many Shepherd drawings in London public collections once formed part of the Gardner and Wilson Collections. When these were dispersed, material from them passed into private hands and has since found its way into a number of private and institutional collections not open to the public. A further unspecified number of drawings have probably never belonged to any major collection.

Bibliography

Although the major dictionaries of artists from Redgrave onwards mention the Shepherds, the references to them are so brief and in many cases inaccurate that there would be no virtue in listing them. There are, however, three recently-published works which are more useful:

Abbey, J. R., *Scenery of Great Britain and Ireland in Aquatint and Lithography, 1770–1860* (Curwen Press, London 1952, reprinted in 1972); includes bibliographical descriptions of some of the Shepherds' rarer publications.

Barley, Maurice, *A Guide to British Topographical Collections* (Council for British Archaeology, 1974); lists many collections holding Shepherd drawings.

Hardie, Martin, *Water-colour painting in Britain* (Batsford, London, 1966–8, 3 vols); mentions the Shepherds only in passing, but indispensible for general reference.

Publications in which the Shepherds' work appears

The following chronological lists are not necessarily exhaustive. All the books listed were published in London; an asterisk indicates a work containing a large number of Shepherd illustrations.

GEORGE

Select Views of London (Vernor and Hood, 1804/5)
Britton, J. and Brayley, E. W., *The Beauties of England and Wales*, Xiii.2 and X.4 (Vernor and Hood, 1810–15)
*Wilkinson, R., *Londina Illustrata* (1811–25)
European Magazine (1810–12)
Ackermann, R. *History of Westminster Abbey* (1812)
Repository of the Arts (1813–15); plates reissued in Papworth, J. B., *Select views of London* (Ackermann 1816)
Dugdale, J., *The New British Traveller* (1819)
*Clarke, C., *Architectura Ecclesiastica Londini* (J. Booth, 1820)
Whittock, N., *The Picturesque Beauties of England and Wales* (1828, 1830)
*Ireland, W. H., *History of Kent* (G. Virtue, 1828–30)

THOMAS HOSMER

*Ackermann, R., *Repository of the Arts* (1809–15, 1820s)
Wilkinson, R., *Londina Illustrata* (1813–25)
Travels of Cosmo the Third . . . Through England (J. Mawman, 1821)
Hassell, J., *Excursions of Pleasure* (1823)
*Shepherd, T. H., *Metropolitan Improvements* (Jones and Co., 1827–30)
*Shepherd, T. H., *Modern Athens* (Jones and Co., 1829–30)
*Shepherd, T. H., *Bath and Bristol . . . Displayed* (Jones and Co., 1829)

*Shepherd, T. H., *London in the Nineteenth Century* (Jones and Co., 1830–31)

*Johnstone, C. M., *The Public Buildings of the City of London Described* (J. Harris, 1831)

*Partington, C.F., *National History and Views of London* (1835)

Tombleson, W., *Tombleson's Thames* (1835)

Fearnside, W. G. and Harral, T., ed., *The History of London* (*c.* 1840)

**London Interiors* (J. Mead, 1841–44)

Dugdale, T., *England and Wales Delineated* (J. Tallis, *c.* 1841)

*T. H. Shepherd, *The World's Metropolis, or Mighty London* (Read and Co., 1854)

Appendix

Prospectus announcing further volumes in Jones and Co.'s series (printed on back cover of No. 26 of *Metropolitan Improvements*, issued September 1828; Guildhall Library):

Notice. Mr. T. H. Shepherd begs respectfully to inform the Subscribers to the present Work, that having just completed his Drawings of the Architectural and Picturesque Objects of the Cities of EDINBURGH AND DUBLIN, he purposes proceeding with the ENGLISH UNIVERSITIES, GREAT COMMERCIAL AND MANUFACTURING CITIES, SEA-PORT TOWNS, FASHIONABLE WATERING PLACES &c. The whole of which will be Drawn and Engraved uniformly with the present Work, and appear in regular succession as early as possible: and at the same time pledges himself that no attention or assiduity shall be wanting to render the whole correct, and worthy of the high patronage and approbation he has already experienced from every quarter, both professional and otherwise. Dublin, Sep. 13, 1828.

Thomas Hosmer's advertisement for a pupil (printed on back cover of No. 40, 19 December 1829; Guildhall Library):

Advertisement. To Parents and Guardians of Youth. Mr. Thomas H. Shepherd, the Artist engaged on the present Series of Illustrated Works, is desirous of taking, as a pupil, a youth of good education and respectable connexions; and, if possessing a taste for the art, will be preferred. A Premium will be expected. Apply (if by letter, post paid) to No. 26, Chapman Street, Liverpool Road, Islington.

Notes

Abbreviations:
GLRO, Greater London Record Office (London Records).
CC, British Museum, Department of Prints and Drawings (Crace Collection).
GL, Guildhall Library.

1 Death certificate
2 Holborn Board of Guardians: Admissions to Workhouses 1875–77; GLRO
3 Register of Baptisms, St Luke, Old Street, which gives the date of birth as 16 January; GLRO
4 His drawings show a continuing interest in this area
5 1851 census (2 Bird's Buildings)
6 CC, portfolio 25, no. 103
7 1851 census (40 Upper Seymour Street)
8 24 Grafton Street (1808), 31 Hertford Street (1809), 18 Carburton Street (1811); Royal Academy lists of exhibitors
9 Drawings in Bedfordshire County Record Office and other collections
10 Drawing in Department of Prints and Drawings, Victoria and Albert Museum
11 The Bonham Carter album of prints and drawings (University of Reading: Museum of English Rural Life, Document Collection) contains drawings by George dated as follows:
   1819, July: 10, Coley Park, Berks; *16*, Reading Abbey Gate; *18*, Aldermaston; *19*, Padworth; *21*, Speen, Donnington; *24*, Hungerford.
   October 8, Faringdon. *1819 (no precise date)*, Whiteknights, Reading; Langley Hall, Berks; Hampstead Park, Berks
   Banbury Reference Library holds a sketch of Banbury dated 1819, from which a sepia drawing was made in 1820 (now in Banbury Museum). Three more drawings from the same series, of Charlbury, Chipping Norton and Witney, were included in Catalogue 82 (1972), issued by Stanley Crowe, 5 Bloomsbury Street, London WC1
12 CC, portfolio 38, no. 37
13 In a private collection
14 Register of Baptisms, St Mary Islington, 3:9:1820, gives the date of birth; GLRO
15 Islington ratebooks, Islington Local History Collection
16 GL
17 Although *Modern Athens* and *Bath and Bristol . . . displayed . . .* appeared in 1829, the sketches for them must have been made in 1827, since surviving dated sketches for *Metropolitan Improvements* and *London in the Nineteenth Century* show that Thomas Hosmer was in London during February, May and July 1828; by mid-September he had reached Dublin. This does not leave enough time during 1828 for the other sketching journeys, which cannot have taken less than two months. There is a significant gap in dated London drawings during the last nine months of 1827
18 See Appendix.
19 Birthdates of Thomas Hosmer's children:

Frederick Napoleon	8:6:1819	St. Mary Islington, Register of Baptisms;
Jane Maria	24:4:1821	GLRO
Emma Caroline	1824/5	Death certificate 5:12:1847
Thomas Hosmer	1825/6	Death certificate 18:11:1848
Rosalie	1833/4	Ages as given in 1851 census (2 Bird's
Valentine Claude	1835/6	Buildings)—probably under-estimated
Helen	1837/8	

20 Birthdates of George Sidney's children:

Percy B.	1832/3	Ages as given in 1851 census (40 Upper Seymour
Stanfield	1834/5	Street); if they are correct George Sidney's marriage
Fanny H.	1837/8	took place *c.* 1831

21 Archives of Federation of British Artists, 17 Carlton House Terrace, London, W1

22 St Pancras rate books, Camden Local History Collection

23 Unpublished notes on family history in the possession of Mr N. K. Crace

24 Post Office directories of the 1850's also list a *James* Shepherd, artist, at 13 Brunswick Street—either a misprint or a further, otherwise unknown member of the family

25 GLC Print Collection

26 Drawings of Crace's home, Vine Cottage, Blythe Lane, Hammersmith (30:8:1854) and his daughter's house nearby (June 1855), both in the collection of Mr Peter Jackson

27 At 5 Cloudesley Street, not far from Brunswick Street (death certificate, registered by Frederick)

28 Finsbury Local History Collection

29 According to the distinguished London antiquary Philip Norman, I. D. Crace was told by his father Frederick that George and Thomas Hosmer were father and son. Norman's comment: 'This is rather strong evidence, but I am still doubtful' (*Notes and Queries*, 1919–20)

30 *Spectator*, no. 69

31 The original copies are in the British Museum (Dept. of Manuscripts, Add. Ms. 33767B). Only two of Thomas Hosmer's redrawn versions are known, this and a view of Newmarket in the collection of Captain Jack Gilbey, but the remaining aquatints are so similar in style that it seems probable that Thomas Hosmer executed all the drawings and perhaps the aquatinting as well

32 *Survey of London*, vol. xxII, p. 93

33 Mayhew, H. and Binny, J. *The Criminal Prisons of London* ... 1862, pp. 232–233

34 *Quarterly Review*, vol. 82, 1847, pp. 142–152

35 Mayhew and Binny, *op. cit.*, p. 96

36 Unidentified cutting in GLC Print Collection

37 *Watercolour Painting in Britain*, vol. 3, pp. 14–15

38 Other contributors to Clarke's *Architectura Ecclesiastica Londini*. Pearson's *landscapes* are reminiscent of Girtin, and much finer than his architectural drawings

39 CC, portfolio 33, no. 63

40 In the collection of Captain Jack Gilbey

41 Greater London Council Library

42 Both in the collection of Mr Peter Jackson

Index

Ackermann, Rudolph, *senior*, publisher, 9, 10, 28, 36, 44
Ackermann, Rudolph, *junior*, publisher, 13
Addison, Joseph, 28
Agricultural Hall, Islington, 86
Albion (Balfe) Street, King's Cross, 13
Aldgate Pump, 72, *37*
Aleph (William Harvey), 16
Alhambra, Leicester Square, 74, *38*
Alleyn's Almshouses, 8, 70, *36*
Almhouses, 8, 70, 76, *36*, *39*
Anachronistic drawings by Shepherds, 38
Apothecaries, 22
Architectura Ecclesiastica Londini, 103
Artificial stone, 26

Bacon, John, sculptor, 26
Bagnigge Wells, 53, *23*
Balfe Street, 13
Balicourt Place, St John Street Road, 13
Banbury, 9, 103
Banking, 16, 22, 62
Banqueting House, Whitehall, 38
Barges, 32, 46, 82
Barker, Thomas and Henry, artists, 96
Batchelor Street, Islington, 10
Bath and Bristol . . . displayed . . ., 11
Bedfordshire, 8, 9, 103
Belle Isle, pottery at, 94, *49*
Binny, John, author, 70
Bird's Buildings (Colebrooke Row), Islington, 12, 14
Bluck, J., engraver, 10, 36
Boswell, James, 58
Boulogne, 10
Boys, T. S., painter, 106
British Museum, *3*, *4*, *8*, *13*, *15*, *32*, *34*, *36*, *38–40*, *48*
Britton, John, antiquary and author, 11
Browne, Sir Thomas, 22
Brunswick (Reid) Street, Islington, 14
Brunswick Theatre, 56, *25*
Bucklersbury, 22, *5*
Bull and Mouth Inn, 30, *9*
Bunyan's Meeting House, 50, *20*
Burford's Panorama, 58, 96, *51*
Burton Street, 13

Caernarvonshire, 10
Camera obscura, use by T. H. Shepherd, 48
Canals, 30, 46, *17*
Canonbury Tower, 48, *18*
Carlyle, Thomas, 82
Caron's Almshouses, Vauxhall, 76
Chad's Row, Gray's Inn Road, 13
Chapman Street, Islington, 10, 12
Charing Cross, 58, *27*
Charles I, statue of, 58
Charles (Mortimer) Street, Marylebone, 13
Chelsea Embankment, 82
Chelsea Local History Collection, *42*
Cheyne Walk, 82, *42*
Churches and chapels, 8, 16, 20, 32, 46, 48,

50, 54, 58, 62, 94, 102, *4*, *12*, *17*, *19*, *20*, *24*
City Basin, Regent's Canal, 46, *17*
City Press, 16
City Road, 8
Clare Market, 35, 103, *11*
Clarendon Square, Somers Town, 9, 11
Clarendon (Werrington) Street, 9
Cleaning and dyeing, 50
Coaches, 16, 28, 30, 36, 44
Coffee houses, 16, 90
Compleat Angler, The, 90
Coade and Sealy, 26
Crace Collection, *3*, *4*, *8*, *13*, *15*, *34*, *36*, *38*, *51*
Crace, Frederick, interior designer and collector of London topography, 14, 15, 66, 70, 76, 105
Crime and punishment, 18, 24, 68, 80, 88
Cromwell, Oliver, 90
Cruikshank, George, artist, 24, 53
Cubitt brothers, 53

Dairies, 22, 64
Dance, George, *junior*, architect, 24
Daniel, George, author and collector, 107
David Copperfield, 32
Devon, 10
Dickens, Charles, 24, 32, 40
Diorama of London, 4
Drury Court, 54, *24*
Drury Lane, 20, 54, 103, *3*
Dublin, 11, 12
Duncan, Edward, painter, 13

Edinburgh, 11, 12
Elmes, James, architect and author, 11
Entertainment, 20, 35, 53, 56, 62, 74, 96, *3*, *23*, *25*, *29*, *38*, *51*
Etchings, outline, 24, 36, *6*, *12*
Euston (Melton) Street, 9
Eversholt Street, 13
Ewer Street, Gravel Lane, 84, *43*
Excursions of Pleasure . . ., 10
Execution Dock, 78
Executions, 24
Exeter Hall, exhibitions at, 13
Extra-illustration, 103, 107, 108, 109

Farren, Percy, theatre manager, 56
Farrington Street, 18
Finsbury, *see* Islington and Finsbury
Fires and fire-fighting, 20, 28, 64, *3*
Fitzroy Square, 9
Fleet Market, 18
Fleet Prison, 18, 88, *2*, *47*
Fleet River, 68, *34*
Fleet Street, 58, 62, 66, *28*, *31*
Fowler, Charles, architect, 64
France, 8, 10
French Horn Yard, Holborn, 66, *32*
Fry, Elizabeth, 24
Fuchsias, 78

Garden Row, Islington, 86, *45*
Gardner, John Edmund, collector of London

topography, 15, 76, 107
Garrick, David, 53
Garrick Street, 98
Gentleman's Magazine, 11
Gibbs, James, architect, 36, 58
Gloucester Lodge, Regent's Park, 56, *26*
Golden Cross Inn, 44, 58
Goldsmith, Oliver, 48
Gordon Riots, 18
Gravel Lane, Southwark, 50, 84, 94
Gray's Inn Road casual ward, 8
Great Britain Illustrated, 12
Great Exhibition, 13, 14, 70
Great Globe, Leicester Square, 74
Greater London Council Print Collection, *2*, *5*, *6*, *10*, *18*, *21*, *23–5*, *33*, *37*, *43*, *45*, *47*, *50*
Greaves family, 82
Guildhall Library, *1*, *7*, *9*, *11*, *14*, *20*, *29*, *31*, *44*
Gun Dock, Wapping, 78, *40*
Gun Tavern, Buckingham Gate, 88, *46*

Haghe, William, painter, 13
Halfway House, Kensington Road, 80, *41*
Hammersmith, Crace's home at, 15
Hampstead Water Company, 44
Hardie, Martin, art historian, 102
Hardwick, Philip, architect, 56
Harvey, William (Aleph), 16
Hassell, John, artist and drawing-master, 10
Haunted House, Gravel Lane, 94, *50*
Havell, William, artist and engraver, 10, 28
Hertfordshire, 8, 103
Hoare's Bank, Fleet Street, 62, *28*
'Holbein' Gate, Whitehall, 38
Holborn, 50, *21*
Holland, Henry, architect, 20
Hollar, Wenceslaus, 38, 90
Holy Trinity, Cloudesley Square, 94
Hone, William, bookseller, 24
Hotels and inns, 30, 58, 66, *9*, *32*
Humours of the Fleet, The, 18
Hungerford, 9
Hungerford Market and Stairs, 32, 64, *10*, *30*
Hungerford, Sir Edward, 32
Hunt, Leigh, 44

Illustrated London News, 66
Industry, 12, 20, 26, 46, 76, 84, 94, *7*, *49*
Insurance, 16
Irish, 84
Islington and Finsbury, 8, 9, 10, 12, 14, 15, 20, 46, 48, 53, 70, 86, 94, *4*, *17*, *18*, *22*, *23*, *36*, *45*
Islington Local History Collection, *22*
Ivybridge, Devon, 10

Jarman, Edward, City surveyor, 28
Jeffreys, Judge, 78
John Bull, 62
Johnson, Dr Samuel, 58
Jones and Co., publishers, 11–12
Jones, Inigo, 38

Kean, Edmund, actor, 35
Keats, John, 44
Kensington Local History Collection, *41*
Kensington Road, 80
King Street, Westminster, 90, *48*

Laurentian Library, Florence, 38
Leicester Square, 74, 96
Le Sueur, Hubert, sculptor, 58
Lighting, 16, 22, 36, 44
Linnell, John, artist, 94
Lloyd's, 16
Lodging houses, 68, 84, *33*
Lombard Street, 16, *1*
London as it is, 106
London Directory, 16
London Interiors, 12, 105
London in the Nineteenth Century, 11–12, 48, 104–5, 108, *18*, *19*
London (Pennant), 103, 109
Londina Illustrata, 10, 38, 103, 104
Louis XVI, 8
Loutherbourg, P. J. de, painter, 96
Lowestoft Lighthouse, painting by G. S. Shepherd, 13

Maiden Lane, 94
Malton, Thomas, *junior*, artist and engraver, 102
Markets, 32, 35, 40, 64, 86, 98, *11*, *14*, *30*, *44*
Mawman, Joseph, publisher, 38
Mayhew, Henry, journalist and author, 64, 68, 70
Melton Street, 9
Metropolitan Board of Works, 66, 98
Metropolitan Improvements, 10, 11–12, 46, 48, 104, 108
Microcosm of London, The, 88
Mighty London, 14
Modern Athens, 11–12, 108
Morning Chronicle, The, 68
Mortimer Street, 13
Museum of London, *12*, *17*, *27*, *30*, *35*

Nash, John, architect, 46, 58
National Gallery, 58
National History and Views of London, 12, 105
Newbery, John, publisher, 48
Newgate Prison, 24, *6*
New Society of Painters in Watercolours, 13–14
Nollekens, Mrs., 44

Old Bailey, 24, *6*
Oliver Twist, 40
Onslow, Arthur, 48
Oxfordshire, 9, 103

Panoramas, 96
Papworth, J. B., architect and author, 104
Paris, 11
Partington, publisher, 12, 105
Peel, Sir Robert, 58
Pennant, Thomas, antiquary and author, 103, 109
Penny Magazine, The, 12, 62, *29*
Pepys, Samuel, 16, 90
Photography, 50
Piccadilly Circus, 30, 44, *15*
Picturesque Tour through London and Westminster, A, 102
Picturesque Tour on the Regent's Canal, A, 10, 46, *17*

Pimlico, 88
Plague, 90
Plan of London, 98, 99–100
Pope's Head Alley, 16
Porters, 18, 36, 58
Pottery at Belle Isle, 12, 94, *49*
Primrose Hill, 62, 103
Princess Theatre, Oxford Street, drawing of, 14
Prior Bolton, 48
Prisons, 18, 24, 70, 88, *2*, *6*, *35*, *47*
Public Buildings of London, The, 11
Public houses, 50, 66, 80, 88, *41*, *46*
Pugin, A. C., artist, 11, 88, 102

Queen's Hotel, 30

Rag gatherers, 68
Railways, 13, 46, 64, 94
Randall's tile kilns, Maiden Lane, 12, 94, *49*
Ratcliff Row, City Road, 9, 20
Read and Co., publishers, 14
Reading, 9
Regent Circus, 44, *15*
Regent's Canal, 10, 46, *17*
Regent's Park, 56, 62, *26*, *29*
Religio Medici, 22
Repository of the Arts, 9, 104, 105, *6*
Richard Street, Islington, 10
Rowlandson, Thomas, artist, 88
Royal Academy, 9, 10, 11, 13, 36
Royal Exchange, 28, *8*
Ruskin, John, 96
Rye, 9

Saffron Hill, 68
St Bartholomew's Hospital, 40, 86
St Dunstan, Fleet Street, 62
St John, Smith Square, 48, *19*
St John Street, Clerkenwell, 13, 15, 86
St Luke, Old Street, 8, 20, 46, *4*, *17*
St Luke's Workhouse, City Road, 8, 53
St Martin-in-the-Fields, 32, 36, 58
St Martin's-le-Grand, 30
St Mary-le-Strand, 36, 54, *12*, *24*
St Mary Woolnoth, 16
St Pauls' Terrace, Camden Town, 12
Select Views of London, 104
Sewers, 66, 68, *31*, *34*
Shaftesbury, Lord, 68
Shepheard, George, artist, 102
Shepherd, Emma Caroline, 12, 14, 114
Shepherd, Fanny, 13, 114
Shepherd, Frederick Napoleon: birth, 10; childhood, 86; career, 14, 15, 64, 66, 88, 107; illness and death, 8, 15; anachronistic drawings, 38; ? self-portrait, 88, *47*; style and technique, 107; drawings, *22*, *30*, *31*, *45*, *47*, *50*
Shepherd, George: career, 8–9, 10–11, 56, 102–3; anachronistic drawings, 38; style and technique, 102–3; signatures, 26, 102; drawings, *1–3*, *5*, *7*, *9–11*, *16*, *26*
Shepherd, George Sidney: early career, 9, 10–11, 103, 106; marriage and later career, 12–14, 94, 106; anachronistic drawings, 38; style and technique, 40, 94, 103, 106; drawings, *14*, *23*, *24*, *27*, *29*
Shepherd, James, 114
Shepherd, Jane Maria, *senior*, 10
Shepherd, Jane Maria, *junior*, 12, 14, 114
Shepherd, Nancy, 8, 9

Shepherd, Percy and Stanfield, 13, 114
Shepherd, Thomas Hosmer, *senior*: birth and childhood, 8, 20; early career, 9–10, 50, 103–4; marriage, 10; works for Ackermann and Jones and Co., 9, 10, 11–12, 104–5; advertises for pupil, 12, 112; later career, 12, 14–15, 105; collaborates with Frederick, 14, 64, 66, 107; erratic spelling, 72; death, 15; style and technique, 48, 76, 80, 102, 103–5; signatures, 104, 106; as engraver, 24, 104–5; drawings: series, 70, 86, 88, anachronistic, 38, comic, 103, self-portraits, 3, 10; plates *4*, *6*, *8*, *12*, *13*, *15*, *17–21*, *25*, *28*, *29*, *32–44*, *46*, *48*, *51*, *52*
Shepherd, Thomas Hosmer, *junior*, wood engraver, 12, 14, 114
Shepherd, Valentine Claude, wood engraver, 14, 15, 98, 114
Shepherdess Walk, Islington, 53, *22*
Sheridan, R. B., 20
Sherman, Edward, coach proprietor, 30
Shops and stalls, 16, 18, 22, 28, 35, 40, 44, 50, 54, 64, 72, 86, 90, 96, *11*, *21*, *30*
Sketches by Boz, 24
Slums, 68, 84, *33*, *34*, *43*
Smithfield Bars, 86, *44*
Smithfield Market, 40, 86, *14*, *44*
Society of Arts, 8
Society of British Artists, 11, 12, 13, 94
Soldiers, 36
Somers Town, 9, 10
Somerset House, 36
Southwark, 50, 84, 94
Stadler, J. C., engraver, 10
Stow, John, historian, 22, 78
Strand, 36, 54, *12*
Street-sellers, 16, 18, 40, 58, 70
Survey of London, 22, 78

Tenter grounds, 50, 84
Theatre Royal, Drury Lane, 20, 35, 103, *3*
Timber-framed buildings, 50, 72, 84, 86, *9*, *10*, *20*, *24*, *33*, *37*, *41*, *43*, *44*
Transport, 28, 30, 36, 44, 46, 58, 62, 78, 82, 94, *6*, *9*, *17*, *40*
Travels of Cosmo the Third . . . through England . . ., 38
Turner, J. M. W., 36
Tyburn, 24

Upper Seymour (Eversholt) Street, 13

Vale of Health, 44, 103
Victoria and Albert Museum, 16, *49*

Waggons, 30, *6*, *9*
Wapping, 78
Warren, Jonathan, blacking manufacturer, 32
Well Street, 56
Werrington Street, 9
West, H., artist, 105
West Street, Saffron Hill, 68
Westminster City Libraries, *19*, *26*, *46*, *52*
Wharves, 26, 46, 78, 82
Whitehall, 38, 90
Wilkins, William, architect, 58
Wilkinson, Robert, publisher, 10, 38, 104
Wood engraving, 12, 14, 62, 66

York Road, 94

Zoar Street, Gravel Lane, 50
Zoological Gardens, Regent's Park, 62, *29*